Ornamental Iro

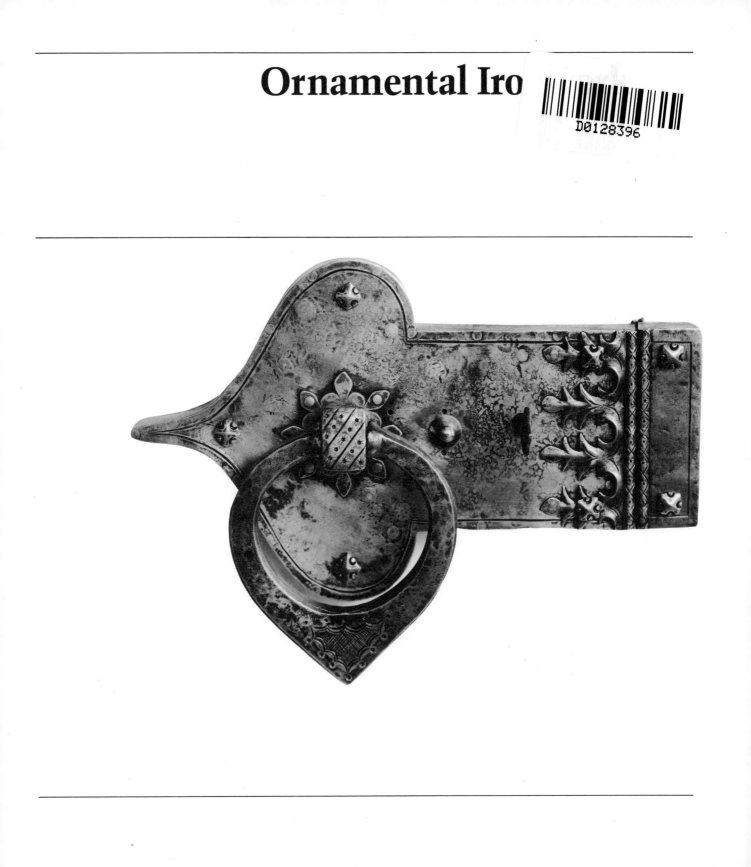

Ornamental Ironwork

An Illustrated Guide to Its Design,
History & Use in American Architecture

By Susan and Michael Southworth
Photographs by Charles C. Withers

McGraw-Hill, Inc.

New York St. Louis San Francisco Auckland Bogotá
Caracas Lisbon London Madrid Mexico Milan
Montreal New Delhi Paris San Juan São Paulo
Singapore Sydney Tokyo Toronto

Library of Congress Catalog Card Number: 91-26936

First published in 1978 by David R. Godine, Publisher, Boston.

1 2 3 4 5 6 7 8 9 0   HAL/HAL   9 7 6 5 4 3 2 1

ISBN 0-07-059804-5

The sponsoring editor for this book was Joel Stein, the editing supervisor was David E. Fogarty, and the production supervisor was Thomas G. Kowalczyk. Design by Logowitz + Moore Associates. Drawings by Richard Hill and James Lombardi.

Printed and bound by Arcata Graphics/Halliday.

Photo on first unnumbered page is hardware for Princeton Chapel by Samuel Yellin, Princeton, New Jersey, 1928. (Photo courtesy of Samuel Yellin Metalworkers Co.).

Illustration facing the title page by permission of the Houghton Library, Harvard University.

This Book is Dedicated
to the
Memory
of
Charles C. Withers
Photographer and Friend

Contents

Foreword

For years the myriad patterns of iron fences, balconies, and door and window grilles have delighted us in the urban landscape. The South has a distinguished tradition of ironwork, most notably the lacelike cast iron verandas of New Orleans, the exquisite wrought iron gates of Charleston, and the iron railings curving up the elegant divided stairways of Savannah. While Philadelphia's historic homes display wrought iron of characteristic simplicity and dignity, Galveston's Ashton Villa is an elaborate Victorian fantasy in cast iron. In New York City, original architectural ironwork can still be found in some neighborhoods such as Gramercy Park, Washington Square, Chelsea, Brooklyn Heights, and Cobble Hill, though it has been less well protected than New York's cast iron buildings. And in California, the great Samuel Yellin created elaborate repoussé doors and forged iron hardware for the Crocker estate in Pebble Beach. The largest collection of original nineteenth-century wrought and cast iron can be found on the streets of Boston's historic Back Bay, Beacon Hill, and South End districts. Here one finds not only fences, gates, and window guards, but balconies, hitching posts, boot scrapers, lanterns, and roof crestings, all in enormous variety.

Our own experience designing ironwork began when the time came to secure the windows and doors of our first Boston residence. What pattern should be used? How would the window and door grilles look from indoors? Would they be strong enough? How much would they cost? How should they be attached to the masonry walls? Who could we find to fabricate them? Each move to a new home gave us the opportunity to explore other styles of ironwork appropriate to the architecture. Upon moving to the San Francisco Bay area one of our first gestures toward personalizing our Mediterranean style house was again ornamental ironwork. This time we designed several massive window guards to protect and enhance ground-level windows; one of them is designed to display potted plants at our breakfast window. We especially enjoy an elaborate gate of intertwined lilies and leaves that mimics the wall of ivy next to it. A dragon atop the gatepost holds a forged bell in its tongue for the postman to announce parcel deliveries. In all of our residences the ironwork has been more than a means of household defense. In New England winters it caught the snow; in summer, it was festooned with morning glories and moonflowers. Throughout the year we have enjoyed the iron patterns that vignette our outdoor views. It has been a continuing delight.

Ironwork imparts a quiet richness and variety to buildings and can enhance visual unity and coherence in neighborhoods. Used on windows and doors for security, along stairs and in fire escapes for safety, and around yards and flower beds for privacy and protection, ironwork is more than just decorative. It can provide a rare architectural opportunity to combine a useful function with a material of extraordinary esthetic possibilities. It is as appropriate on contemporary as on historic architecture.

During the 1970's and 1980's interest in historic preservation grew enormously, along with an enthusiasm for architectural ornament and ironwork. Until recently it was difficult to find craftsmen with high-level skills in working iron, but today there appears to be a revival of the art. Artisans can be found in nearly every part of the country who are capable of producing high-quality and creative forged or cast ironwork. Artist-blacksmith organizations have formed throughout the country and creative work in iron is widely exhibited and published. This rebirth of interest in ornamental ironwork has encouraged us to prepare a new edition.

This book emphasizes the design of ironwork and its role in architecture and the urban landscape. We are concerned with contemporary ironwork as well as with historic restorations or reproductions. While this is neither a history book nor an artisan's manual, we have tried to include both source material on ironwork history and some insights into various techniques. Iron architecture is outside our domain, despite the many wonderful iron gazebos, columns, and cast iron facades that have struggled for consideration. Numerous examples of American architectural ironwork have been selected that are representative of several cities, principally Boston, Charleston, Chicago, Galveston, New Orleans, New York, Philadelphia, Pittsburgh, Savannah, and Washington, D.C., but examples from California and other areas are also included. From the thousands of pieces across the country we have of course been able to take only a small sampling. Several patterns of both historic and contemporary design are offered for use and adaptation by the homeowner, architect, and blacksmith. These have been selected with particular consideration given to their design qualities and relative ease of fabrication. Ironwork Resources (Chapter 10) has been completely updated and expanded to include resources such as organizations, museums, journals and books, and suppliers of blacksmithing materials.

We are grateful to the many people who have contributed to the realization of this book. Without the assistance of the late Charles Withers, our loyal and patient photographer and great friend, our project would have been impossible. His energy kept us on schedule and was invaluable in the laborious task of searching out and photographing hundreds of specimens throughout the country. His bonhomie won invitations to photograph private courtyards and even motivated one Charleston lady to climb out upon her upper balcony to remove a rumpled newspaper that compromised a view. Margaret Craver Withers has offered much valuable advice drawn from her extensive experience as an artist working in metals. Albert Paley spent several hours discussing his outstanding ironwork with us and provided several photographs. Eric Clausen, an artist-blacksmith in Oakland, California, has not only shared his knowledge of forging techniques, but has helped us locate other creative artist-blacksmiths working on the West Coast today. The late Harvey Z. Yellin enthusiastically showed us the Samuel Yellin Museum in Philadelphia and generously provided photographs of the Yellin pieces reproduced here. Today his daughter, Clare Yellin, continues to operate the workshop begun by her grandfather and has provided us with photographs of Yellin work in this edition. Theodor Hauri read the manuscript and made helpful suggestions on techniques of iron fabrication. Logowitz + Moore, the book's designers, were very responsive to our wishes and created an award-winning design for the book. We also wish to acknowledge the assistance of the Boston Athenaeum, Boston Public Library, Harvard Libraries, Philadelphia Athenaeum, and Pyne Press, as well as the help of the late Bainbridge Bunting, Margaret Floyd, Professor E. N. Hartley of MIT, Judy McDonough of the Boston Landmarks Commission, Sally Pierce of the Boston Athenaeum Prints and Photographs Collection, and Sally Withington. Finally, we thank Joel Stein of McGraw-Hill for his efforts in making the new edition of this book possible.

Susan and Michael Southworth

Ornamental Ironwork

Ornamental Ironwork

Ironwork in Architecture

During the nineteenth century the art of fabricating objects of iron flourished in America. Everything from kitchen equipment and cradles to farm machinery and civic fountains found expression in iron. Among the most enduring works of this period, aside from cast iron buildings, which are beyond the scope of this book, have been architectural and landscape ornaments—the door grilles, window guards, balconies, verandas, and fences that adorn buildings across the country. Although ironwork is appreciated primarily for its decorative value, most of it is functional. More than enhancing gardens, iron fences make obvious definitions of private territory and protect it from damage by intruders. Ornamental window and door grilles serve the crucial function of deterring burglars but still allowing the enjoyment of sun and view. Though ornamental, little early ironwork is frivolous.

Just as iron replaced wood as a material for balconies and verandas in nineteenth-century southern architecture, today, other materials—plastic, fiberglass, aluminum, and concrete—have largely replaced cast and wrought iron. Fences and screens are commonly made of concrete, either poured in place or precast in 'sculptured' blocks. Even more prevalent is that twentieth-century atrocity, the chainlink fence. Today's balconies are typically made of concrete or wood. Planters, urns, and garden ornaments are 'fabricated' of aluminum, fiberglass, or concrete, in confusing varieties.

Despite this onslaught of new materials, the architectural ironwork industry is experiencing a revival. Iron has maintained its value for defensive grillework; in fact, with present concerns for security, it enjoys increased demand. No other low-cost material can substitute for the strength, durability, and relative lightness of iron. In addition, with growing interest in architectural preservation and restoration across the country, property owners and developers seek ironwork replacements, reproductions, and repairs consistent with eighteenth- and nineteenth-century precedents. Thus, ornamental ironwork from demolished buildings no longer languishes in the junkyard but appears in antique shops at stiff prices.

What is ironwork? What does it do? Four basic functions of architectural ironwork may be identified: *ornament, utility, privacy,* and *security.* Most ironwork serves several of these functions simultaneously.

Ornament

Well-conceived ornamental ironwork can upgrade a plain, even ugly, building, while ironwork ornament such as Victorian roof crestings (FIG. 2) can soften the harshness of pure architecture by functioning as the intermediary between the solid building block and the sky. An ironwork fence can introduce buildings to the passersby. On a facade, ironwork can relate windows to wall, create a focus, or enhance the play of light, snow, or rain. Ironwork can also function visually on a larger scale. On streets where the architecture lacks unity, a procession of iron fences, balconies, or lamp posts can establish a rhythm and harmony among varying architectural styles. (FIG. 3)

Fortunately, ironwork is an architectural decoration that is still economically feasible at a time when other types of ornament—cut stone, mosaic, carved wood, or stained glass—are all beyond almost every pocketbook. Moreover, iron is highly durable, unlike wood, painted decoration, plastic, plaster, or stucco. But unfortunately, much contemporary work is little more than utilitarian, a blemish more than an improvement of architecture and neighborhood. Today's iron fabricators no longer have carpenter patternbooks like Asher Benjamin's *Practice of Architecture* (1833) and catalogs of high-quality mass-produced components to draw upon as did their nineteenth-century predecessors. Then too, contemporary ironworkers rarely have the technical capabilities of earlier craftsmen. Nevertheless, successful ironwork can still be created at reasonable prices using simple designs, common techniques, and an eye for quality.

Utility

Much ironwork serves a specific utilitarian function. The fire escape is a good example. (FIGS. 4, 5) We rarely consider its

FIGURE I
Sun and shadow are dramatized by
the beveled scrolls and ribbed leaves
in this cast iron balcony railing. Some
of the spiny leaves almost seem to
represent sea horses. (Boston, 7–9
West Cedar Street; built 1834, Asher
Benjamin, Architect)

Ironwork in Architecture

FIGURE 2

Victorian iron cresting is a delightful yet inexpensive ornament that has great impact on a building and on the city skyline. Its use is generally limited to Victorian architecture. (Boston, 303 Dartmouth Street; built 1876, Shaw & Shaw, Architects)

FIGURE 3
This cast iron balcony follows the bows of the pair of row houses and provides an important decorative addition to the building. Anthemions are paired in heart-shaped scroll frames. Particularly noteworthy are the projecting wrought iron serpents whose twisted tongues and tails form flagpole holders. (Boston, 3 Louisburg Square; built 1846–1847)

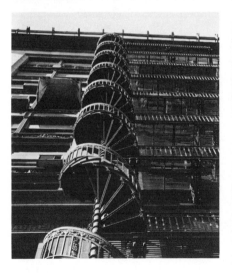

FIGURE 4
Now demolished, this handsome cast iron spiral fire stair was an important element in the architecture. (New England Merchants Bank, Congress Street, Boston.)

FIGURE 5
This fire escape is the outstanding ornamental feature of a simple brick structure. To most passersby it appears to be a decorative veranda. Rungs of the ladder are ornamented with scrolls. (Boston, 3 Brimmer Street; built 1897, John Bemis, Architect)

Ironwork in Architecture

appearance. Most often it runs awkwardly up a building, cutting across windows and obliterating the facade. Balconies and verandas, ornamental at their best, are first of all a means of providing outdoor space above the ground level. Hand rails, balustrades, door hinges, latches, and knockers are other common examples of utilitarian ironwork.

One step removed are iron street furnishings—lamp posts, sign standards, tree guards, drains, hydrants, or benches. The foot scraper and hitching post, utilitarian fixtures of nineteenth-century life, now fall in the ornamental category—except in neighborhoods with excessive dog populations where the foot scraper becomes a welcome necessity! (FIGS. 6a–g)

Privacy

Privacy and the desire to maintain or protect it leads to the installation of fences, screens, or boundary demarcations. Unbounded lawns all too easily come to be considered part of the public right-of-way; fences protect flower gardens and lawns while permitting public enjoyment. (FIGS. 7, 8) Although this protective function in Victorian times was primarily served by decorative iron fences, fencing today is more often of wood, or, less happily, cheap and ugly wire. Iron fences, though strong, need not look like fortresses. A low edging of a foot or two can communicate the boundary, keeping out small animals and even most children. The low edging says, 'This is where my garden begins and the public is to stop.' It may not physically prevent all animals from entering, but it does provide a clear signal to careless feet.

Where semiprivacy is desired, as around a swimming pool or patio, filigree or other densely patterned ironwork can be effective for visual screening. When extended overhead it becomes an arbor, providing a framework for climbing plants and a cool summer retreat screened from full view. The iron framework itself can be a sculptural addition of considerable grace and delight in all seasons. Windows of city houses fronting directly on a sidewalk can benefit from this type of filigree screening (FIG. 9), for it limits public view indoors while permitting light, air, and a view of the outside.

Security

Ironwork is becoming increasingly important for security of windows, doors, yards, and driveways. Preoccupation with security has always been a fundamental concern, evident, for example, in

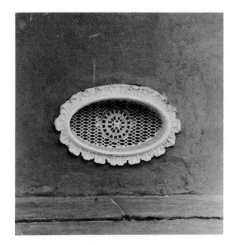

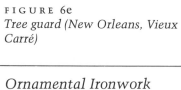

FIGURE 6d
Lamp post (New Orleans)

FIGURE 6e
Tree guard (New Orleans, Vieux Carré)

FIGURE 6g
Downspout (Savannah)

Ornamental Ironwork

FIGURE 7
This unusual example of wrought iron is used in a low edging fence. The ends of short square bars, hammered flat, create a fan-like ornament. Each group of five bars is defined by an arched segment and two circular ornaments. (Boston, 177 Beacon Street; house built 1871, Snell & Gregerson, Architects)

FIGURE 8
Here we have a very charming wrought iron garden gate with some cast elements supported on carved stone posts. The thin, cupped leaves are beautifully formed. The gate is painted an attractive gray-brown color relating well to the brownstone. (Boston, 117 Beacon Street; 1864)

FIGURE 9
This small rounded wrought iron balcony is one of a pair that serves both to enhance the matching windows and to screen the interior from passersby. (Boston, 76 Beacon Street)

defensive ironwork on medieval and Renaissance architecture. As a defensive material iron is still unexcelled, open enough to allow a view of the outside while strong enough to prevent unwanted access. With good design iron can serve both ornamental and defensive functions simultaneously, letting the owner feel secure and ornamented, but not imprisoned. (FIG. 10) Too frequently the defensive rush to protect windows and doors drives people to bypass esthetics and install prison-like grilles that make no concession to architectural style or to the fact that the windows are, after all, windows, intended for comfort and enjoyment. The cost difference between taking the standard prison configuration and choosing a visually pleasing pattern may be minimal, but it represents a vast improvement in value and livability.

FIGURE 10
An iron door with glass set behind it provides a lovely light entrance for a house. It can serve defensive functions while providing natural light in the foyer. Note the iron ornament over the door containing the address of the house. The door check should have been mounted inside the entry. (Boston, 13 Commonwealth Avenue; built 1907, Parker, Thomas, & Rice, Architects)

Techniques of Ironwork

Architectural ironwork is of two basic types, wrought and cast, distinguished both by the way they are formed and the type of iron of which they are made. Wrought iron, the more ancient, is hand forged, while cast iron, a later development, is mass-produced from molds. Wrought ironwork uses iron of lower carbon content (0.04% carbon) than cast iron (2.0–6.0% carbon). Iron with less carbon is more resilient and soft than iron with more carbon, which becomes brittle and hard. Today most 'wrought' ironwork is actually mild steel having somewhat more carbon (0.2–0.6% carbon) than true wrought iron; the high-quality, low-carbon iron used in earlier centuries is difficult to obtain today.

Wrought Iron

The term 'wrought iron' [1] is often misused; it is applied to everything from bent wire to cast aluminum. 'Wrought' literally means 'worked' and refers to the way the iron is formed. Traditional smiths are very particular when they use the term 'wrought.' Many even distinguish it from simple 'bent' iron, which has not received the hammering, stretching, or twisting of a good wrought piece; a 'bent' piece is simply heated and shaped and does not require the hand forging skill of traditional wrought ironwork. Though much attractive and functional work is done in this way, it should not be termed wrought iron. True wrought iron may often be recognized by the sinuous, linear patterns forged from bars. Hammer marks are often evident, and since wrought ironwork is handcrafted, it will have irregularities in the pattern. These are highly valued indications of hand craftsmanship. (FIG. 12)

Wrought ironwork demands the high malleability characteristic of low-carbon iron. It can be hammered out hot or cold. 'Forged work' is done with hot iron worked on an anvil; cold iron is

FIGURE II
Eighteenth-century blacksmith's shop; from engraving in Diderot's Encyclopedie, *Vol. 9, 1771. (Photo courtesy of Boston Public Library)*

FIGURE 12
This fine example of wrought iron scrollwork uses flat, ribbon-like strips of iron. (Charleston, S.C., Kahal Kadosh Beth Elohim Synagogue, 74 Hasell Street; 1838, C. L. Warner, Architect)

worked at the bench and is called 'bench work.' Under heat, iron bends readily and can be stretched, compressed, or bent back upon itself without breaking. It is not brittle and has high tensile strength. The more it is worked, however, the more dense, brittle, and hard it becomes. When broken, its fibrous structure is visible. Because of its low carbon content, wrought iron is less susceptible to rust than any other type. Swedish iron, considered the finest for wrought ironwork, is not generally available today; it is the lowest in carbon content, and of all iron it is the easiest to work, the toughest, and the least susceptible to rust. Today mild steel has largely replaced wrought iron because it is less expensive. It is somewhat more difficult to use for elaborate hammered work and rusts more readily than wrought iron, but it can be bent and welded easily. The travesty of adding hammer marks to make factory-formed mild steel bars appear hand forged should be avoided.

Production of Iron

Wrought iron is now usually produced in two stages. Iron ore is first smelted in a blast furnace with layers of coke and limestone. Formerly, enormous quantities of charcoal were used in the smelting process. In England, so much timber was consumed in making charcoal that whole forests were threatened until in 1558, an act was passed to limit deforestation; ironworks of violators were demolished. Raw coal, too inflammable and impure to use in smelting, was not a suitable substitute for charcoal. Not until 1713 was the process for turning raw coal into coke developed by Abraham Darby, the Quaker ironmaster of Coalbrookdale, England. Coke produced the high heat necessary for iron smelting and enabled the iron industry to flourish.

Once melted, the iron is drawn off into molds, called sows and pigs. This picturesque terminology apparently was inspired by the arrangement of the molds, which resemble several pigs surrounding the sow. (FIG. 13) As the molten iron hardens, the impurities float to the surface—leaving 'pig iron,' which then must be 'puddled' before becoming wrought iron. Puddling is a process patented in 1784. The pig iron is remelted at 2,100° F., boiled and stirred until most impurities have burned. Then it is 'frozen' or hardened and squeezed to remove further impurities, leaving a 'bloom' of wrought iron, a spongy mass that can be hand hammered or machine rolled into a variety of forms.

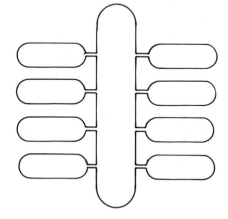

FIGURE 13
Sow and pigs, molds used in making "pig iron."

Techniques and Tools

Wrought ironwork techniques fall into three broad classes. BLACKSMITHERY uses forging techniques. (FIG. 14) In LOCKSMITHERY, less ancient than blacksmithery, wrought iron is worked in a cold state by filing, drilling, chiseling, and sawing; it is used primarily in locks; fretwork is a decorative application of this technique. Finally, there is REPOUSSÉ, in which thin sheets of iron or other metal are pounded out from the back, then the front, to create an embossed or bas-relief effect. Lead is usually used as a base in forming repoussé work. Jean Tijou, the great French smith who worked in England in the late seventeenth and early eighteenth centuries, brought this difficult technique to its artistic peak in iron masterpieces of incredible ornateness. (FIG. 15)

Of the three, blacksmithery is by far the most common technique used in architectural wrought ironwork. Some of the common tools of the art include *hearth* and *bellows,* for heating the iron; *hammers,* for shaping it; *anvil,* a steel block on which iron is hammered; *vise* and *tongs,* used for holding and handling the iron. A *swage* is a die for shaping metal by hammering, and a *fuller*—the opposite of swage—is used for making indentations. *Hot and cold sets* or *chisels* split or cut iron; *punches* make holes or marks; *drifts* open out and smooth holes. A *mandrel* is used for forming iron rings; *files,* for smoothing iron; and *saws* and *shears,* for cutting iron. (FIG. 16)

Five levels of heat are used in wrought ironwork, each level being progressively hotter. *Dull* or *blood red heat* is sufficient for finishing previously forged surfaces; *bright red heat* permits simple bends and hot chisel work. *Yellow heat* is used for main forging—drawing out and scroll work, for example. *Full welding heat* is needed for welding mild steel; *white heat,* hottest of all, is required for welding pure wrought iron.

Some basic blacksmithery techniques include *bending, incising* (to engrave patterns into the iron with a burin), *scrolling, splitting, punching,* and *welding. Drawing out* is a technique that lengthens the iron bar and makes it more slender; *jumping* or *upsetting,* the opposite of drawing out, shortens the iron bar and makes it thicker. (FIGS. 17a, b)

Wrought iron connections are often made by hammered welds, in which the pieces of iron are heated to the point of fusion and

Techniques of Ironwork

FIGURE 15

Although of bronze, this scenic door is included because it illustrates the repoussé technique, a technique Yellin also used in iron. Yellin's name and the date are seen behind the ring. A metal flap covers the keyhole to the left of the handle. (Repoussé bronze door by Samuel Yellin, Mrs. Templeton Crocker residence, Pebble Beach, California; George Washington Smith, Architect, 1927) (Photo courtesy of Samuel Yellin Metalworkers Co.)

Techniques of Ironwork

FIGURE 16

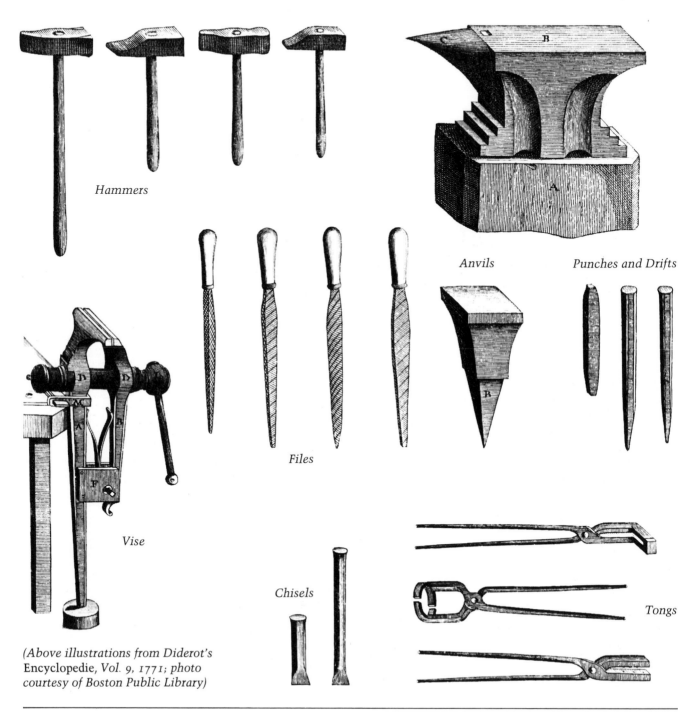

Hammers

Anvils

Punches and Drifts

Files

Vise

Chisels

Tongs

(Above illustrations from Diderot's
Encyclopedie, Vol. 9, 1771; photo
courtesy of Boston Public Library)

Flattening   *Jumping or Upsetting, to shorten and thicken the bar.*

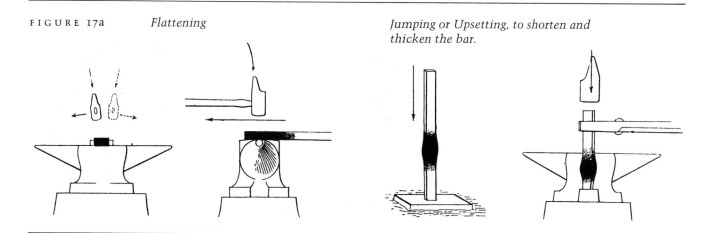

Drawing out, to make the bar longer.

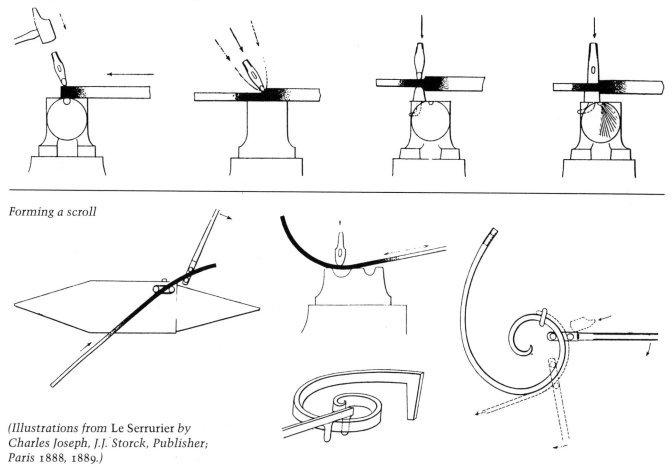

Forming a scroll

(Illustrations from Le Serrurier *by Charles Joseph, J.J. Storck, Publisher; Paris 1888, 1889.)*

FIGURE 17b
These door handles, elements of a complete ensemble of hardware for a residence, illustrate Yellin's use of incising to create decorative patterns. (Wrought iron by Samuel Yellin, Mrs. Templeton Crocker residence, Pebble Beach, California; George Washington Smith, Architect, 1927) (Photo courtesy of Samuel Yellin Metalworkers Co.)

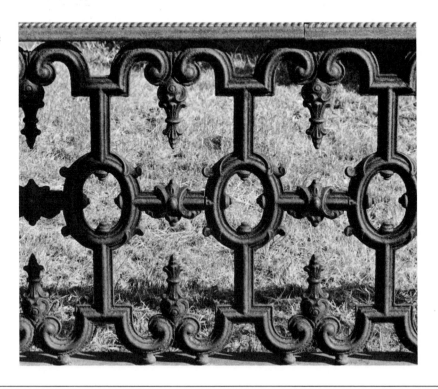

FIGURE 19
An example of open mold casting; the back side of the fence is blank. Such extravagant—some would say decadent—baroque patterns satisfied the eclectic Victorian longing for complexity. (Boston, 11 Union Square)

hammered together. Other wrought iron connections include the rivet, collar or band, pin, screw, and bolt. (FIG. 18) Torch and arc welds, modern timesaving variants of the hammer weld, are frowned upon by smiths adhering to traditional methods, but they are used almost universally in contemporary work. Although strong and economical, they lack the personal touch of hammered welds and are frequently disfigured by lumps or pits.

Cast Iron

Cast iron,[2] as its name implies, is made by being poured in its liquid state into molds. Because it is molded rather than hand forged, it is far better suited to mass production than wrought iron. Usually, it is quite easily recognized; cast iron components have great uniformity, unlike most wrought ironwork, where irregularities are evident. (FIG. 19) Cast iron patterns are often one-sided and have a rough back, having been cast in a one-sided or open mold. Cast iron is usually more massive than wrought iron and can never achieve the filigree quality or the hand-tooled appearance of fine wrought ironwork. Nor can it take the detail of bronze; iron does not flow as freely into the mold. Frequently, cast iron has a rough surface caused by a coarse sand mold or by mold burns from the molten iron.

The high carbon content of cast iron makes it brittle, weak in tension, and more subject to rust than wrought iron. However, cast iron is more resistant to fire and has the high compressive strength that makes it suitable for columns; hence its use in much nineteenth-century 'cast iron architecture.' Though it cannot be hardened, cast iron machines easily. Since it is more difficult to weld than wrought iron, a nickel-cadmium rod must be used; otherwise, it may be brazed, with brass as the bonding metal.

With a technology far more elaborate than that of wrought iron, cast iron is inappropriate for small industry or local blacksmiths. It employs three trade groups: pattern makers, molders, and founders. As with wrought iron, manufacture of cast iron begins with pig iron. This is remelted, usually in a furnace called a cupola. Pig iron alone is usually considered too soft, so cast iron scraps are added. As more scrap iron is mixed in, castings become harder.

Liquid iron is then poured into molds of two general types, open and closed. Open molds are usually formed on the foundry floor and are one-sided, the upper surface being unformed and exposed

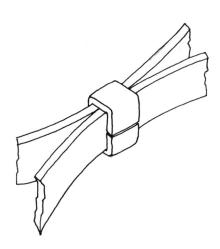

FIGURE 18
Collar connection

Techniques of Ironwork

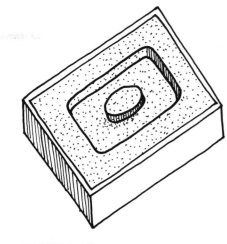

FIGURE 20
Open mold

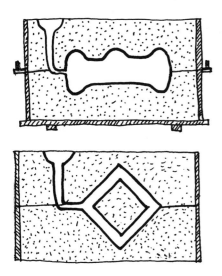

FIGURE 21
Closed mold

to the air. (FIG. 20) Closed molds are made of two or more parts that fit together to enclose the iron completely. (FIG. 21) Complex patterns may require molds of several pieces so that castings may be removed without damage to the mold. Most often made of sand, molds may also be made of other earths or metal. Metal molds are usually used where durability is essential for mass production.

The original mold pattern is usually made of wood, most often yellow pine or mahogany, but plaster of paris or metal patterns may also be used. Patterns must take account of the shrinkage of cast iron—about ⅛ inch per foot upon hardening. A sand mold is made by packing the sand into an iron frame called a flask. The quality of sand is critical to the end result; the sand may be either dry or 'green' (moist). The pattern is then pounded into the sand with a sledge hammer. For a two-piece closed mold, another flask is added on top and rammed with sand around the projecting pattern. The lower part of the mold is called the 'drag' and the upper half the 'cope.' Open molds are usually made in green sand; closed molds are either green or dry. Dry sand molds are more suitable for heavy castings, being harder and more resistant to the heavy flow of molten iron. In the making of a dry sand mold, the green sand mold is baked in an oven. Large molds are reinforced with bars to prevent breakage. Because of their weight, castings must often be hollow, and a core mold is used for these. In effect, another mold, or core, is placed inside the closed mold, causing the iron to flow in a thin layer between the core and outer walls of the mold.

A casting is made by pouring molten iron into the mold through a hole called a 'sprue.' Air must escape through another hole on the opposite end called a 'riser.' When very large castings are made, 'pit molds' are usually used. The mold is placed in a pit beneath the foundry floor to protect workmen in case the mold breaks when the molten metal is poured. When the iron is hardened, it is taken from the mold and cleaned. Sand and irregularities caused by the flow of iron into sprues, gates, or risers are removed.

3 American Ironwork: an Historical Sketch

In America, production of wrought and cast iron on an industrial basis began in 1644 at Lynn, Massachusetts (now in Saugus) with the establishment of an ironworks called Hammersmith. Although there had been earlier attempts at establishing ironworks in the colonies, none had been successful. John Winthrop, Jr., son of Governor Winthrop of Massachusetts, started the Hammersmith project by obtaining about twenty-five London investors and a team of experienced ironworkers, mostly Scottish prisoners sent over after the defeat at Dunbar. Located on the Saugus River, which provided water power and a means of transport, Hammersmith had a furnace, forge, rolling and slitting mill, storage facilities, workmen's housing, and a pier for small boats. (FIG. 22) Early cast iron products included pots and hollowware, anvils, weights, and firebacks. Wrought iron products included hinges, shovels, hoes, and spades. Poor management, along with the high cost of processing bog ore, led to the eventual failure of Hammersmith (ca. 1670). It did, however, set the pattern and provide the personnel and experience for numerous subsequent ironworks that spread throughout the colonies, many operated by Hammersmith ironworkers or their descendants.[3]

Wrought Ironwork

Early architectural wrought ironwork in the colonies was produced by local blacksmiths who spent most of their time fabricating items of utility—horseshoes, tools, cooking utensils, boot scrapers, or hardware such as hinges, locks, and latches. More elaborate architectural ironwork—window guards, fences, balconies, or gates—was produced, but its cost usually limited it to fine homes, public buildings, churches, parks, and cemeteries.

A smith's advertisement in the *South Carolina Gazette* (Charleston) of 21 May 1753 indicates the range of his skills:

JAMES LINGARD, Smith and Farrier, makes all kinds of scroll work for grates and stair cases; ship, jack, and lock work, and all other kinds of smith's work at his shop on Mr. *Maine*'s (commonly called *Frankland* or *Sinclair*'s) wharf. Gentlemen that employ him, may depend on having their business done to satisfaction, with all possible despatch, and at the most reasonable rates.—N.B.—He will take care of gentlemen's horses, and see that they have good care in case of sickness. JAMES LINGARD.'[4]

An earlier listing in a similar vein appeared in the *Boston News-Letter* of July 6–13, 1732:

BLACKSMITH'S WORK. This is to give Notice, that there is one William Bryant, Blacksmith, that now keeps a shop adjoining to the Presbyterian Meeting House in Long Lane, Boston, who makes and mends Glazier's Vises, Cloathers' Screws, and worsted Combs, and makes, grinds, and setts Cloathers' Shears; he also makes and mends Smiths' Vises, Ship Carpenters', Blockmakers', Tanners', Glovers' and Coopers' tools, Braziers' and Tinsmen's Shears, and makes Housework, with many other things too tedious to mention here. He will make and engage his work to any of his Employers according to the value of them.'[5]

FIGURE 22
The Saugus Ironworks, founded in 1644 at Lynn, Massachusetts on the Saugus River, contained a rolling and slitting mill, forge, blast furnace, warehouse, and ironmaster's house (right to left). (Photograph by Richard Merrill)

Early American wrought ironwork is understandably most prevalent in eastern and southern cities—principally, Boston, New York City, Philadelphia, Washington, D.C., Charleston, Savannah, and New Orleans. Styles and methods were largely derived from European precedents, particularly English. In Savannah in the 1700s, groups of planters are said to have commissioned European craftsmen to come and teach talented slaves the art of ironwork.[5] It is probably safe to infer that much of the early work in Savannah, and perhaps in other parts of the South as well, was done by blacks.

In Charleston, Savannah's neighbor and rival in architectural ironwork, St. Michael's Church commissioned a wrought and gilded communion rail in England in 1772. This imported rail must have inspired local ironworkers, for its design motifs frequently appear in other local work.[6] Even in the nineteenth century, the three outstanding ironworkers in Charleston were European: J. A. W. Iusti, Christopher Werner, and Frederick Julius Ortmann, all German.[7]

Stylistic Influences in Early Ironwork

As in England, the classical revival style, part of the larger English romantic movement, greatly influenced ironwork design in America during the late eighteenth and early nineteenth centuries. Publication of numerous books of archaeological drawings and designs helped bring about a revival of classical Greek and Roman styles. The first of these books, *The Ruins of Palmyra, otherwise Tedmor, in the Desart* and *The Ruins of Balbec, otherwise Heliopolis in Ceolosyria,* both by Robert Wood, were published in London in 1753 and 1757 respectively. *Antiquities of Athens* by James Stuart and Nicholas Revett followed in 1762. Then in 1764 came the influential *Ruins of the Palace of the Emperor Diocletian at Spalatro in Dalmatia* by Robert Adam, a Scottish architect regarded as the leading force behind the classical revival. Both Robert Adam and John Nash designed much architectural cast iron using new motifs. Ironworkers quickly adopted the classical vocabulary, but they by no means copied the ancient prototypes, using them instead as a source of design inspiration.

Publication of numerous design handbooks with ironwork patterns, first in France, then in England, and finally in America, disseminated ironwork styles and motifs. These handbooks, filled

American Ironwork: an Historical Sketch

with large engravings or lithographs, presented a wide array of designs for the builder and ironworker to copy or adapt. The earliest known English ironwork publication, *A new Booke of Drawings* by Jean Tijou, the great French repoussé ironworker, was published in 1693 preceding the onset of the classical revival. (FIG. 23) A strong French influence is also found in later English handbooks. Popular English ironwork handbooks of the eighteenth and nineteenth centuries included these:

J. Jores; *A new Book of Iron Work,* London, 1756.

William and John Welldon; *The Smith's Right Hand or a Complete Guide to the Various Branches of all Sorts of Iron Work Divided into Three Parts,* London, 1765.

J. Bottomley; *A book of Designs,* London, 1793.

I. and J. Taylor; *Ornamental Iron Work,* London, ca. 1795.

Lewis Nockalls Cottingham; *The Smith and Founders Director,* London, 1824.

Henry Shaw; *Examples of Ornamental Metal Work,* London, 1836.

FIGURE 23

*The repoussé technique, especially appropriate for the ornate style of the late 17th-early 18th century English ironwork, is illustrated in this piece by Jean Tijou, the great French smith. Tijou worked in England between 1689 and 1712. (*A new Booke of Drawings, *by Jean Tijou, 1693. By permission of Houghton Library, Harvard University.)*

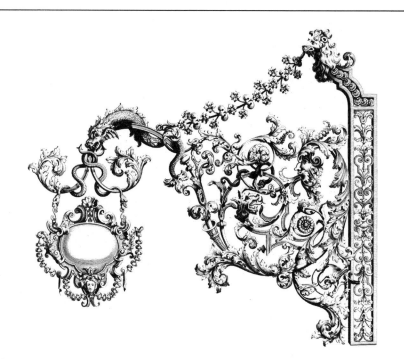

Ornamental Ironwork

Of the English handbooks, Cottingham's *Smith and Founders Director* is particularly rich and has several patterns seen in America (F I G. 24), including the cast iron fence at 12 Arlington Street and elsewhere in Boston. (F I G. 25)

One of the most influential handbooks in America was Asher Benjamin's *Practice of Architecture,* first published in Boston in 1833. Benjamin issued a series of these tremendously successful guides treating all phases of building ornament from plaster work to ironwork. (F I G. 26) Three of his patterns (*Practice of Architecture,* Plate 60, 1833 edition) can be seen today on Boston's Beacon Hill, at 91 Pinckney Street, 73 Hancock Street, 2 Joy Street, 41 West Cedar Street, and 44 Beacon Street. (F I G. 27) Patterns in these handbooks were first adopted in cast iron in major American coastal cities in the decade 1830–1840; between 1840 and 1850 they rapidly spread to inland areas.

Cast Ironwork

Cast iron is less ancient than wrought iron. Although bronze and gold have been cast since antiquity, iron could not be cast until a process had been developed to generate the high temperature required to melt it. The first known dated example of cast iron is a lion made in China and dated 11 September 502 A.D. The earliest known European cast work dates from the fifteenth century, but architectural cast iron reached England only in the early eighteenth century, when a cast iron fence was erected (with Wren's strong disapproval) around St. Paul's Cathedral (1710–1714). In England, the cast iron industry developed between 1750 and 1820 and flourished between 1820 and 1860. Although it took time to reach America, by 1840 or 1850 cast iron had largely taken the place of wrought iron, and by the 1860's cast iron was being produced at three to four times the rate of wrought iron. In Boston alone, employment in the iron industry tripled between 1845 and 1855.[8] The cast iron era came to an end in the 1880's and 1890's with the introduction of steel.[9]

With the advent of cast iron in the nineteenth century, architectural ironwork became available throughout most of the country. Cast iron producers first appeared in the North in Boston, New York, and Philadelphia and later moved South and to the Midwest. Many companies began by making utilitarian items such as stoves and furnaces and then expanded into more decorative work. Most of the companies produced wrought as well as cast

FIGURE 24

Cast iron patterns from Cottingham's
Smith and Founders Director *first pub-*
lished in London in 1824. (Photos by
Barry Donahue; by permission of The
Houghton Library, Harvard Univer-
sity)

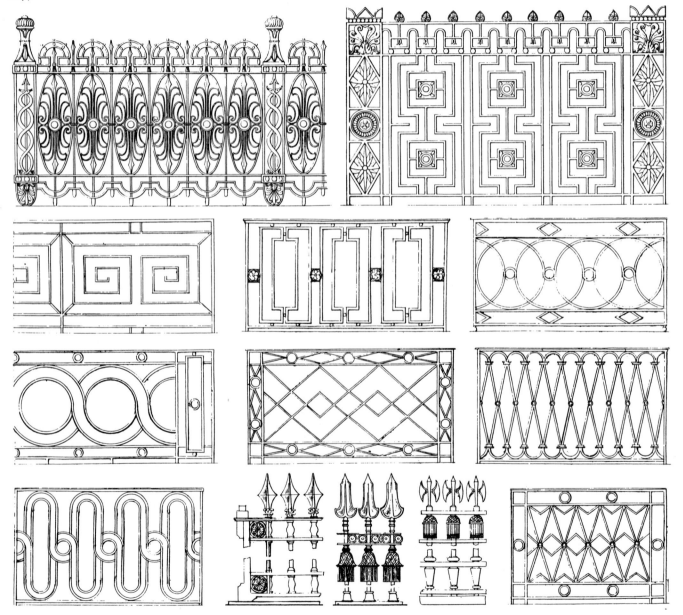

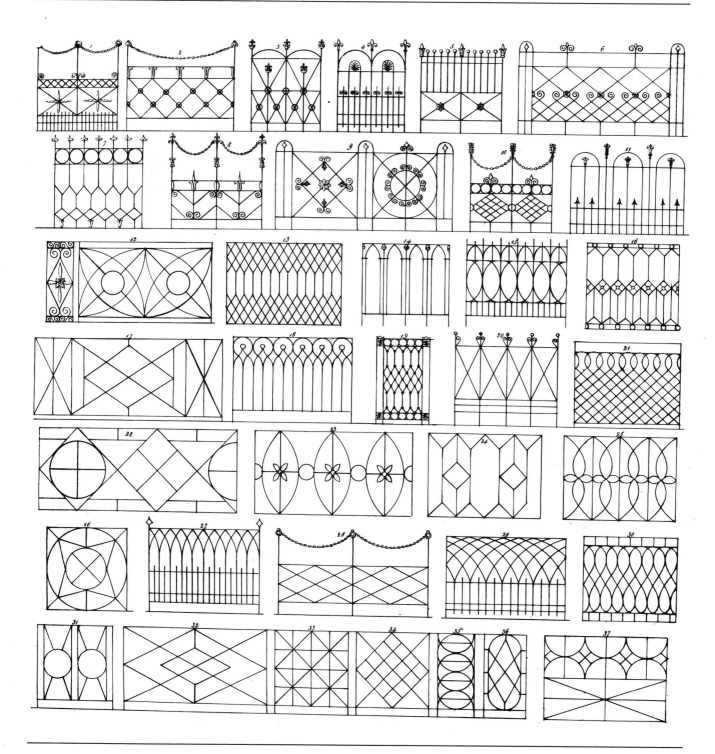

American Ironwork: an Historical Sketch

FIGURE 25
Of purely geometric pattern, this cast iron fence could have been created in the twentieth century. The pattern actually first appeared in L. N. Cottingham's Smith and Founders Director *(1824) and became a popular Victorian pattern in America. Despite the fact that the composition is all curves, there is no sense of the florid or exotic. It could be used as a source of inspiration for contemporary bent iron designs. (Boston, 12 Arlington Street; built 1860, Arthur Gilman, Architect)*

FIGURE 26
Cast iron patterns from Asher Benjamin's influential design handbook can still be seen in Boston. (Plate 60, Practice of Architecture, *1833 edition. Photo courtesy of Boston Athenaeum.)*

FIGURE 27
Cast iron rarely attains the wrought iron-like lightness seen in this balcony. A simplified version of anthemion alternating with lotus is the theme. The cast iron fence and stair rail use an anthemion and scroll pattern. Both patterns are found in Asher Benjamin's Practice of Architecture *(1833). (Boston, 75 Hancock Street; nineteenth century)*

American Ironwork: an Historical Sketch

iron. Cast iron could be mass produced, was readily sold through catalogs and transported in parts. Items illustrated in catalogs were ordered by number, then shipped by train to almost any region of the country. As an example of prices, one 1876 catalog offered roof cresting for $1.38 per foot, and six-foot lengths of three-foot high fencing for $13.30. Cast iron often replaced wood fences, balustrades, or balconies that were in poor condition or simply out of fashion. An 1895 advertisement of Hinderer's Iron Fence Works (New Orleans) boasts 'Iron Fences cheaper than wood.' The first cast iron patterns were based on earlier wrought iron designs, but new patterns in the eclectic Victorian styles soon appeared. These tended to be heavier than the classical revival designs. Patterns encompassed the classical revival and the many facets of the Victorian movement, including 'rustic,' oriental, and Gothic themes.

Catalogs

Victorian cast iron catalogs provide a feast for eyes subsisting on austere modern architecture. The 1858 catalog of Wood and Perot, a Philadelphia company, is particularly lavish, a massive book illustrating hundreds of items. Designs are often fantastic— even ugly; they were influenced by the English romantic movement. One cast iron cemetery fence, for example, was designed to look like interlaced budding branches. Just as the twentieth century has exploited plastic, the Victorians made everything they possibly could of iron. The Wood and Perot Catalog contains not only dozens of fence, gate, and grille designs, but also garden pagodas, fountains, urns, statuary, beds, cradles, garden furniture, balconies and verandas, trellises, lanterns, and cistern canopies. (FIG. 29)

The Victorians have often been criticized for attempting to imitate flowers, logs, lace, and other materials in iron. Unlike wrought iron, cast iron has little integrity as a material. No one form is more 'appropriate' than another in cast iron, which can take the form of nearly any mold. This plasticity creates an advantage in production, but a disadvantage in design, for it gives most designers more freedom than they can control. Thus, to many tastes today, much Victorian production seems frivolous, wild, and even fraudulent. But after the austerity of the Bauhaus, appetites for the decorative and romantic are reviving; the fantastic decoration of our Victorian grandparents is becoming fashionably collectible.

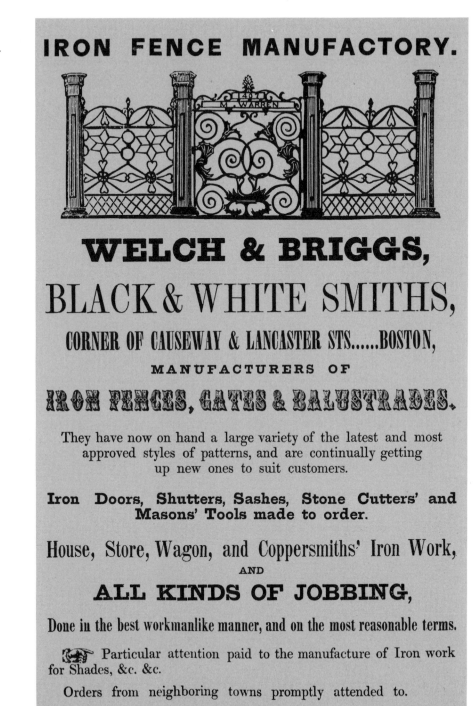

American Ironwork: an Historical Sketch

No. 201.
WOOD & PEROT, Philadelphia,

No. 202.
WOOD & PEROT, Philadelphia,

American Ironwork: an Historical Sketch

FIGURE 30
Winslow Brothers, a 19th century Chicago ironwork company, fabricated ironwork for a variety of uses. The influence of art nouveau and of Louis Sullivan is seen in much of their work. These elevator enclosures are shown in their catalog of 1894. (Photo courtesy of Boston Athenaeum.)

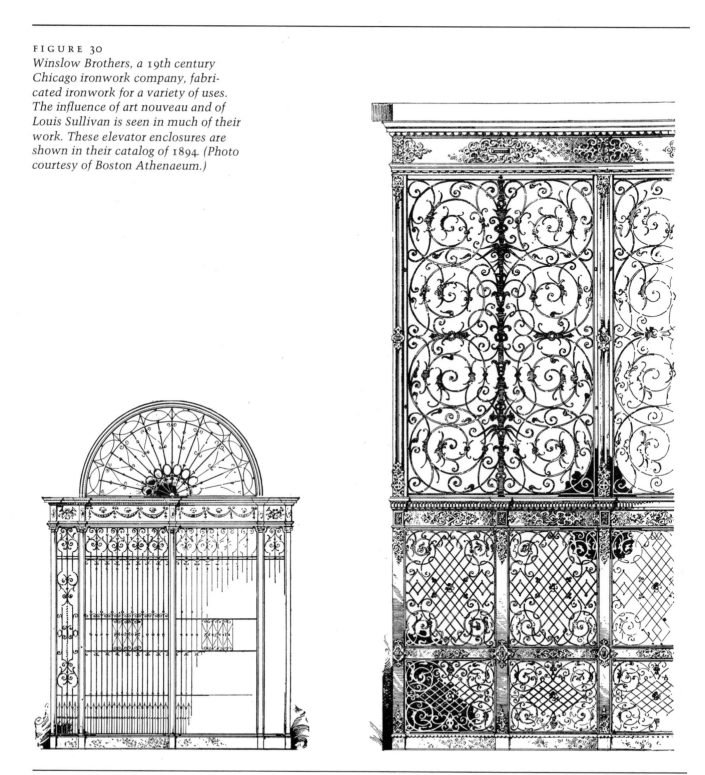

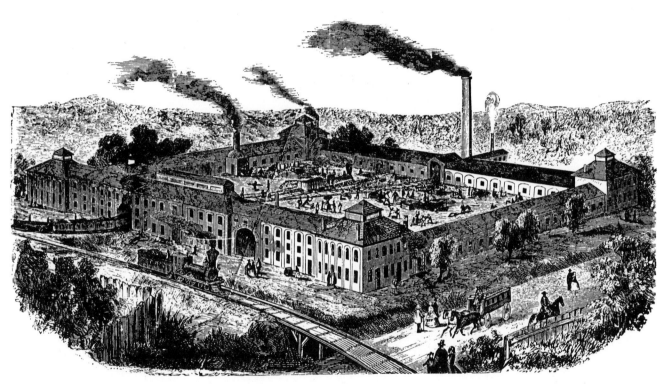

VIEW OF THE IRON WORKS OF JANES, KIRTLAND & CO., NEW YORK.

FIGURE 31
continued

Ornamental Ironwork

Tree Guards

American Ironwork: an Historical Sketch

Design Motifs in Historic Ironwork

Most historic patterns fall into two broad categories of motifs: geometric and plant.

GEOMETRIC MOTIFS

Greek key	Heart
Scroll (Vitruvian, Greek wave, and Rinceau)	Trident
	Lozenge
Circle or circular segments	Wave
Herringbone	Cross
Woven strips	Spiral or twist
Square	Star
Gothic arch	Ball
Trefoil	Round arch
Quatrefoil	Diamond

PLANT MOTIFS

Anthemion (also called Greek honeysuckle or palmette)	Rose
	Leaf
Acanthus	Tulip
Husk festoon	Wreath
Laurel	Sunflower
Lotus	Acorn and oak leaf
Lily	Tropic passionflower
Grape vine or grape clusters	Bamboo
Fleurs-de-lis	Garland
Pineapple	Branches
Corn	

OTHER MOTIFS

Lyre	Violin
Georgian shell	Pelican
Columns (fluted and plain)	Griffin or gargoyle
Urn	Pegasus
Portraits or figures	Initials
'Sea lions' or sea horses	Tassels
Spear, arrow, or spike	Arrow and wheel
Coronet	

The anthemion, sometimes called Greek honeysuckle or palmette, was a favored motif in ironwork inspired by the classical revival. The Greek key, acanthus leaf, lotus, husk festoon, urn, Georgian shell, columns (fluted and plain), and lyre are also common in classical revival work. To this repertoire, Victorians added 'new' motifs—the Gothic arch, bamboo, fantastic creatures such as griffins and gargoyles, and a plethora of plant forms. Some

FIGURE 32

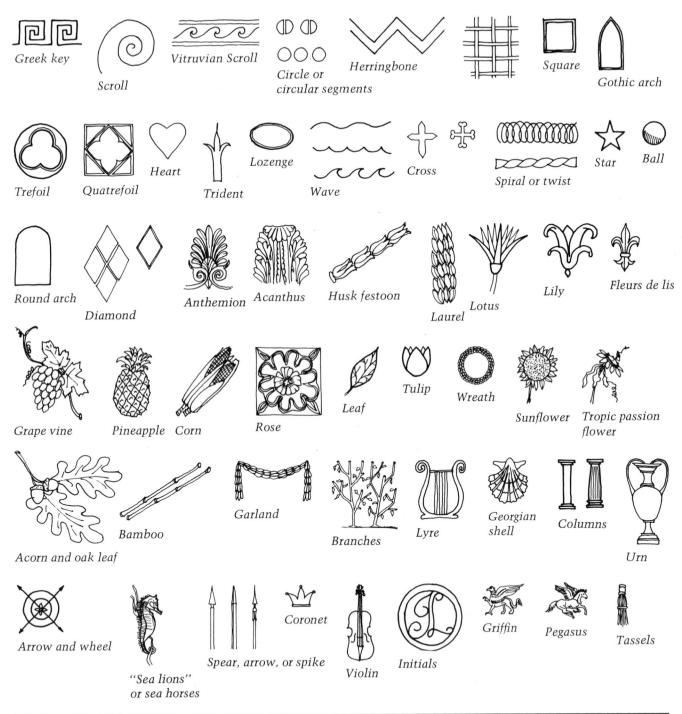

Greek key

Scroll

Vitruvian Scroll

Circle or circular segments

Herringbone

Square

Gothic arch

Trefoil

Quatrefoil

Heart

Trident

Lozenge

Wave

Cross

Spiral or twist

Star

Ball

Round arch

Diamond

Anthemion

Acanthus

Husk festoon

Laurel

Lotus

Lily

Fleurs de lis

Grape vine

Pineapple

Corn

Rose

Leaf

Tulip

Wreath

Sunflower

Tropic passion flower

Acorn and oak leaf

Bamboo

Garland

Branches

Lyre

Georgian shell

Columns

Urn

Arrow and wheel

"Sea lions" or sea horses

Spear, arrow, or spike

Coronet

Violin

Initials

Griffin

Pegasus

Tassels

regions, particularly the South, represented indigenous flora in ironwork. The passionflower and grape vine are common motifs in New Orleans. In Galveston the corn husk became a decorative motif in the fanciful and admirably preserved cast iron fence posts of Ashton Villa. (FIG. 33) The tradition of using native flowers continues even today. One delightful example is the sunflower gate in Savannah at 345 Habersham Street where giant iron sunflowers welcome visitors at the front door. (FIG. 34)

One of the most characteristic decorative motifs in traditional ironwork is the scroll, a common form that is more than just decorative, for in much old work it provides crucial diagonal bracing, keeping gates and fences from sagging. (FIG. 35) Forming a scroll properly demands great skill and distinguishes the amateur ironworker from the expert craftsman. A finely worked scroll spirals gracefully in evenly modulated increments with the iron becoming thinner toward the innermost point of the scroll. (FIG. 36a) Much scroll work produced today is a travesty of the concept. Ends are bluntly hacked off, and instead of a continuous smooth curve we see an awkward series of bends. (FIG. 36b) Numerous types of scrolls are to be found, including: ribbon end, fish tail end, snub-end, fish tail snub-end, halfpenny snub-end, bolt-end, leaf-end, and beveled. Composite scrolls are the 'C' scroll and the 'S' scroll. (FIG. 37)

Another basic decorative motif found in both old and new work is the twist. Twists are usually formed by placing the hot iron bar of square or rectangular cross section inside a pipe and twisting the ends in opposite directions, the pipe restraining the bar from longitudinal bending. Bars may also be twisted cold in a lathe.

The Problem of Identifying Ironwork Dates and Makers

Unfortunately for historians, most smiths, like medieval artisans, worked anonymously. Few signed their work, considering it more craft than art. Thus it is difficult to identify specific makers and dates. One is tempted to make deductions by dating the architecture to which ironwork is attached, but this too can be misleading. Ironwork was often added long after buildings were constructed; the date of the building establishes only the earliest likely date for the ironwork. Federalist houses, for example, were often 'modernized' by adding nineteenth-century Victorian iron balconies or verandas. To confound the problem even more, it is known that ironwork was frequently taken from a demolished

FIGURE 33
FIGURE 34
FIGURE 35

FIGURE 33
The cornstalk is a motif in the fanciful cast iron fence of Ashton Villa in Galveston. The pattern is found in Wood & Perot's 1858 catalog.

FIGURE 34
The sunflower theme makes these handwrought gates more than merely a security device. (345 Habersham Street, Savannah. By Ivan Bailey Metal Studio, Atlanta, Georgia.)

FIGURE 35
Besides being ornamental, scrollwork can provide diagonal bracing.

American Ironwork: an Historical Sketch

FIGURE 36a *(right)*
A well-formed scroll flows in smooth curves with the flat iron becoming thinner in the center.

FIGURE 36b
The contemporary scroll most often looks like misshapen wire.

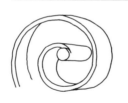
Bolt-end

'C' scroll

Fish tail end

Fish tail snub-end

Ribbon end

Snub-end

FIGURE 37
Types of Scrolls

Halfpenny snub-end

Blow over leaf

FIGURE 38
This elaborate cast iron balcony is said to be from the Tuileries Palace Catherine de Medici began in Paris in 1564. It is not to be assumed that the railing necessarily dates from the construction of the Palace. It was removed from the Tuileries after the Palace was burned in 1871 during the Paris uprising. In 1885 it was installed on this Back Bay house. The same house has two other iron patterns worth noting: the intricate filigree balconies of the second floor and the contrasting massive and simple ground floor window guards made from round bars (see Figure 128). (Boston, 32 Hereford Street; built 1884, McKim, Mead, & White, Architects)

building and re-installed on other structures. An extreme example is the balcony said to be from the Tuileries Palace in Paris, begun in 1564 by the architect Philibert de l'Orme for Catherine de Medici. The balcony was removed after the palace was burned during the Paris uprising of 1874, and in 1885 it was installed on the Victorian Renaissance revival house of John Andrew built in 1884 at 32 Hereford Street, Back Bay, Boston.[10] (FIG. 38)

City directories can be useful in identifying local ironworkers of different periods. Newspaper advertisements, wills, and account books are also good sources of information. Alston Deas, historian of Charleston ironwork, made effective use of these in identifying several early Charleston pieces. Occasionally, names of manufacturers can be found on cast ironwork. Where this is not the case, cast iron catalogs can be helpful in identifying origins and approximate dates. Since competing companies sometimes produced the same patterns, however, one can never be certain of the source, even if the ironwork has been identified in a catalog. Companies often mass produced patterns under their own name after lifting designs from panels purchased from another company. These were, after all, the days before patent protection for designs.

American Ironwork: an Historical Sketch

FIGURE 39
Royal Street in New Orleans exhibits an enormous but unintegrated collection of architectural ironwork.

FIGURE 40
The overall effect of this minimal railing is pleasing in relation to the pale stone facade behind it. However, acanthus leaf scroll posts in cast iron seem far too elaborate for the simplicity of the railing. The pattern could be easily executed today. (New Orleans, 828 Toulouse Street)

4 Regional Ironwork

Regional differences are nationally apparent even within the same period. These variations can be attributed both to local tastes and to the varying capabilities and production lines of individual workshops. Northern work tends to be more restrained and less fanciful than its southern counterparts. In some locations, a particular style of ironwork seems to have captured people's fancy and spread throughout the region. Cast iron balconies and verandas, for example, rare in America before 1840, suddenly began appearing throughout the central and southern states, particularly in New Orleans and Savannah.

New Orleans

The ironwork of New Orleans has a light, lacelike quality that is unique. Early work is attributed to French and Spanish workers.[11] In fact, Stuart M. Lynn states that most of the better wrought iron in New Orleans was actually manufactured in Spain.[12] Unhappily, this early wrought ironwork was destroyed in the fire of 1788. Thus, the majority of extant New Orleans ironwork is nineteenth-century cast iron. Research has shown that much of this was painted bronze or soft, bright green; some fences were even gaily polychromed in naturalistic colors! [13] Of the wrought iron that exists, patterns tend to be simple and delicate, with geometric rather than floral motifs. Examples are the balconies at 828 Toulouse Street and 805 St. Ann Street. (FIGS. 40, 41) Occasionally, balconies are seen with florid initials of the owner in a cartouche worked in wrought iron and placed in a focal position in the composition, as in the balcony of the Roquette Mansion at 411 Royal Street. (FIG. 42) In most cases, the supporting brackets for balconies have been given unusual design emphasis and form an integral part of the total effect.

FIGURE 41
This railing epitomizes the simple delicate wrought ironwork of New Orleans, every detail contributing to the overall design. (New Orleans, 805 St. Ann Street)

FIGURE 42
A medallion panel with the initials of the building's former owner, Domingue Roquette, is the focus for this simple but pleasing early nineteenth-century railing composed of rings and bar segments. Note the double scroll bracket balcony support and the defensive spike clusters on the divider grille to deter entry from the neighboring balcony. (New Orleans, Roquette Mansion, 411 Royal Street)

FIGURE 43
New Orleans is famous for its verandas. Here a cast iron double veranda
supported by slender cast iron columns envelops the entire facade.
(New Orleans, 716 Dauphine Street)

Regional Ironwork

Cast ironwork appeared in the Lower Garden District of New Orleans by 1849, but the cast iron galleries and verandas for which the city is famous were added after 1850. The two-level veranda at 716 Dauphine Street is characteristic. (FIG. 43) At this time cast ironwork also became popular in other southern towns, including Richmond and Savannah. In contrast to the abstract geometric tendencies of New Orleans wrought iron, the cast ironwork of that city usually employs plant motifs. Leaves and vines adorn the railing and spandrels of the Dauphine Street veranda. The feeling remains light and airy, but the patterns are more intricate. Verandas, probably added to the building years after it was built, are supported on slender cast iron posts. Not only did the added-on verandas update the style of older buildings, but they also provided private outdoor space for the upper floors of buildings, much appreciated in this subtropical climate.

Charleston

In Charleston, South Carolina, it is not balconies and verandas but wonderfully beautiful and varied gates that became the local specialty. The work is largely of wrought rather than cast iron. Gates to churches and churchyards may have launched the movement, but now one sees iron gates—wrought and cast—to gardens, front yards, 'sally ports,' driveways, houses, or porches.

J. A. W. Iusti's fine wrought iron gates for St. Michael's Churchyard set the pattern for much later work in Charleston. (FIGS. 45a, b) The top panel of the gates employs the urn motif surrounded by scrollwork while the bottom panels resemble a four-petaled flower composed of scrolls. The gates are made almost entirely of thin, flat strips of iron. Connections are riveted or welded. The scrolls, perfectly formed, are flattened to a thin edge at the center, some terminating with a cast rosette. Surprisingly, the gates were signed on the overthrow by the maker, Iusti, and are among the few signed pieces of old architectural wrought ironwork in America. The urn and flower motifs appear throughout Charleston, the gates of Boone Hall Plantation being one example (FIG. 46), but none equal the design and workmanship of Iusti's St. Michael's gates that inspired them.

St. Philip's Church and Churchyard gates are also noteworthy. (FIG. 47) Although the church gates themselves are relatively simple, employing the popular lyre motifs along with simple geometric ring and bar patterns, the overthrow is quite elaborate,

FIGURE 44
The Vulcan Ironworks or 'Sign of the Anvil' of Archibald MacLeish, active 1830–1850 (Charleston, S.C.; Cumberland Street), displays some of its produce—a veranda and a fantastic found object sign-sculpture—in this nineteenth-century stereopticon view. (Library of Congress B8171–3112)

Regional Ironwork

Made by J. A. W. Iusti in the eighteenth century, these gates inspired many of the fine gates of Charleston. They are one of the few pieces of architectural iron to be signed by the maker. Although they are defensive, their appearance is completely delightful, avoiding common defensive symbols such as spears and prison bars. (Charleston, S.C., St. Michael's Episcopal Church, 80 Meeting Street; built 1752–1761)

Ornamental Ironwork

The urn and scrolls are executed in flat stock with exquisite workmanship. The gates are equally beautiful at all scales, from a distance or under the closest inspection. (Charleston, S.C., St. Michael's Episcopal Church, 80 Meeting Street; built 1752–1761)

Regional Ironwork

FIGURE 46
The central urn and scroll motif panel is obviously based on St. Michael's gates in Charleston (Fig. 45). These gates form the entrance to the walkway leading to the plantation house. (Charleston, S.C., Boone Hall Plantation)

FIGURE 47
An unusual spear cresting between a pair of urn motifs tops the overthrow of this gate, beneath which are palmettes, shells, and then a band of scrolls and further urns. Perhaps most noteworthy are the 'flying buttress' fence supports—found in several Charleston locations—that form an important part of the composition. (Charleston, S.C.; St. Philip's Episcopal Church, 146 Church Street; 1835)

Ornamental Ironwork

having several motifs: urns, spears, shells, anthemions, and scrollwork. The end effect seems more ostentatious and perhaps less harmonious than the St. Michael's gates. The curving fence braces at St. Philip's are another ironwork detail, common in Charleston but rare elsewhere. Braces, normally omitted or treated as purely structural elements, here become part of the overall design, enhancing the fence both visually and structurally.

Another set of handsome Charleston gates are those at 1 Ladson Street. (FIG. 48) The motifs are geometric—scroll and circle—the pattern focusing on an elegant central round latch plate of brass. Guarding the gates, a snarling winged dragon in iron sits atop the pilaster.

Although Charleston's gates are its unique contribution to architectural ironwork, there are also many lovely wrought iron balconies in the city, such as the one at 27 Meeting Street. Using geometric motifs, this exhibits the delicacy typical of most Charleston wrought ironwork. (FIG. 49) The small balcony at 71 Church Street illustrates the rather unusual 'pulpit' style found in Charleston. This early eighteenth-century balcony is simply ornamented with small scrolls and is supported by a single scroll bracket. (FIG. 50)

The round window grille on the City Hall basement, built in 1801 as the U.S. Bank, is another interesting Charleston piece. (FIG. 51) Gabriel Manigault, the architect, worked in the style of Robert Adam. Petal-like loops, surrounded by scrolls, radiate from a small cast iron flower rosette. The lovely grilles on the rear basement windows, instead of being round, are arched and employ a scroll-anthemion pattern, or 'peacock scroll,' one of the earliest applications of the anthemion motif in Charleston. (FIG. 52)

Savannah

Balconies, verandas, and stair rails are the themes of Savannah ironwork. Cast iron predominates, but there are such fine wrought iron examples as the divided stairway on the Davenport House on Columbia Square—now headquarters for Historic Savannah. (FIG. 53) A simple design heightens the effect of the curving double stairway; ornamentation is confined to the central landing. Here scrolls and twists combine to create a delicate geometric flower. And even a foot scraper has been worked into the stair rail near the newel post.

FIGURE 48
The driveway of this house is handsomely protected by these gates. Scrollwork predominates, with palmettes in the outer corners of the circular pattern. Note the semicircular brass latch plates and the small winged dragon keeping watch. (Charleston, S.C.; 1 Ladson Street)

FIGURE 49
Handsome 'S'-scroll brackets support this delicate balcony of interconnected concentric circles, diamonds, and fretwork. (Charleston, S.C.; 27 Meeting Street; post-revolutionary)

FIGURE 50
This early eighteenth-century pulpit-shaped balcony is supported on a single handsome scroll bracket at the center. The restrained scroll pattern of the railing is appropriate for the complex shape of the balcony. (Charleston, S.C.; Col. Robert Brewton House, 71 Church Street; built ca. 1730)

FIGURE 51
This bull's-eye window guard is a prime feature of the Charleston City Hall for passersby. It features the Vitruvian scroll surrounding a simple flower motif. (Charleston, S.C.; City Hall, originally United States Bank, 80 Broad Street; built 1801, attributed to Gabriel Manigault, Architect)

FIGURE 52
The "peacock scroll" window grille on the City Hall is one of the earliest uses of the anthemion motif in Charleston.

FIGURE 53
All of the ornamentation is concentrated on the landing of this double stairway. Despite the plainness of the stair railings, the curves contribute to the overall decorative effect. Foot scrapers are symmetrically inserted in the railing. (Savannah, Davenport House, 324 East State Street; built ca. 1820–1821)

One type of wrought ironwork rarely seen today outside Savannah is of thin wire-like iron about ⅜ inch in diameter. Chase Brothers Catalog Number 15 (Boston, ca. 1859) contains a similar product termed 'Patent Woven Wire Guards.' Such thin stock is, of course, easy to work, requiring little more than bending and welding. An example is the pair of gates at 215 West Charlton. (FIG. 54) The iron 'wire' interlaces and key intersections are fastened with cast iron medallions. Although attractive and economical, this type of ironwork is more subject to damage than heavier forms.

The veranda at 10 West Taylor is one of the many outstanding Victorian cast iron pieces in Savannah. (FIG. 55) An unusual cast iron stairway divides the veranda into two sections. Risers of the stairway are perforated to reduce weight and to allow passage of light. The cast iron pattern is basically geometric, with scrolls and quatrefoils, but some plant motifs are also present. Pieces like this, ordered item by item from catalogs, were assembled on the site.

At 124 McDonough we see several types of catalog ironwork: balcony, veranda, fence, and lamp posts in cast iron and window guards in simple 'woven wire.' (FIG. 56) The ironwork may have been added to the house after it was built, possibly at different times. Several patterns are mixed together, a practice encouraged by cast iron catalogs filled with alternative and interchangeable designs.

Also in Savannah are the unique and comical posts at 4 West Taylor Street. (FIG. 57) Although commonly called 'pelican posts,' they were really intended to be cranes, each standing with one raised foot holding a stone; the raised feet have broken off. According to legend, cranes—symbolic of vigilance and loyalty—gather in a circle around their king to keep night watch. In order to stay awake they stand on one foot, raising the other. If the bird should fall asleep, the stone falls on its other foot and awakens it! Wood and Perot's 1858 catalog illustrates a lamp post (Design 'B') with the same curious and vigilant bird.

Surprisingly, one of the nineteenth-century American ironworkers about whom we know the most was a woman, Juliette (Daisy) Gordon Low, whose only work was a pair of gates. (FIG. 58) A remarkable Savannah socialite and civic leader, she is best

FIGURE 54

Lightweight wire-like stock is woven and fastened with cast iron rosettes, creating a delightful nineteenth-century version of chainlink fence. Contemporary copies of this gate could easily be made. These techniques are much less demanding than those of most wrought ironwork. The ease of duplication in no way diminishes the striking effect this pattern makes in its several locations in Savannah. (Savannah, 215 West Charlton Street)

FIGURE 55

This house has several fine iron pieces including a veranda, corner mounted lamp, and an extraordinary iron stair with perforated iron risers. Note the simple iron columns with leafy capitals supporting the veranda. It is appropriate that they do not try to compete with the bird-cage fragility above. On the rear right, the famous 'pelican posts' can be seen at the base of the stairway (see Figure 57). (Savannah, 10 West Taylor Street; mid-nineteenth century)

Ornamental Ironwork

FIGURE 56
Cast iron fence, balcony, lamp posts, veranda, and wrought iron window guards, all of different designs, are combined in this 'catalog' house. The balcony railing pattern, found in the Wood and Perot catalog, can also be seen on the balcony of the Stoddard-Laughton House in Savannah (Perry Street) as well as in several parts of Boston's South End. (Savannah, 124 McDonough Street)

FIGURE 57
The cranes on this stair rail symbolize vigilance and loyalty. Newel posts are often a focus for personal expression. One post in Boston has a sculpture of the original owner's dog! (Savannah, 4 West Taylor Street; ca. 1850)

FIGURE 58
Juliette Gordon Low, Savannah society girl, iron worker, and founder of the Girl Scouts.

remembered as the founder of the Girl Scouts. At one point she decided that instead of grouse shooting on her Scottish estate, as was her custom, she would devote the summer to producing a pair of gates, now appropriately known as 'Daisy's Gates.' These can now be seen in the garden of Ms. Low's birthplace at the corner of Oglethorpe Avenue and Bull Street in Savannah.[14]

Galveston

Galveston's Ashton Villa, built for James Moreau Brown in 1859, is an elaborate Victorian fantasy in cast iron. (FIG. 59) Again, a number of patterns are boldly combined, including unbelievable corn ear and stalk posts, also used at 1448 Prytania Street in New Orleans. The fence appears in Wood and Perot's catalogs of 1858 and 1860–61, and it was probably manufactured by their New Orleans branch, Wood, Miltenberger & Company. It should be noted that the gates themselves are not of cast, but wrought, iron. The pointed arches of the veranda are supported on slender cast iron columns with oversized Corinthian capitals. Columns are rhythmically spaced in pairs. Acanthus leaf scrolls fill the spandrels. As with so much Victorian cast iron work, it was too easy to do too much; although delightful, the effect may not be one of beauty.

Philadelphia

Consistent with Philadelphia architecture is the restraint of its wrought ironwork. The stair rails at 273–279 Fourth Street illustrate characteristic Philadelphia simplicity and dignity. (FIG. 60) Scrolls, diamond loops, crosses, and rosettes are the only devices used. Despite the simplicity, a whole row of such stair rails enriches the street. The pattern may also be seen in the fine divided stairway at 715 Spruce Street. (FIG. 61) The fence and stair rails at 708–710 Spruce Street are another frequent Philadelphia pattern, combining the Greek key and an 'x' motif. The pattern is in Wood and Perot's 1858 catalog as 'Design Number 59.' (FIG. 62) This pattern was also available with a cresting of cast iron stars identical to those found on another variation of the 'x' motif fence at 270 Third Street. (FIG. 63) From an historical viewpoint the wrought iron main gates of Christ Church at Fifth and Arch Streets are also noteworthy. Although their design is unremarkable, the gates are signed and dated by their maker, 'S. Wheeler—1795,' a rare instance of documented ironwork. The cast iron fence of Philadelphia's Second Bank of the United States, in contrast to the wrought ironwork, is one of the more

Ornamental Ironwork

massive examples of cast iron in the country. (FIG. 65) The anthemion motif, normally treated in a very refined style, becomes heavy and defensive, topped by spikes. Although not entirely satisfying in itself, the ironwork, with its classic Greek motifs, does harmonize with the weighty dignity of the temple-like bank.

Boston

In Boston we see further regional specialization; wrought and cast fences abound, especially in Beacon Hill, the South End, and Back Bay. In addition, Back Bay features door and window grilles. The Back Bay and South End, which comprise one of the largest areas of contiguous Victorian architecture in the country, are ideal study grounds for Victorian enthusiasts. Much of the South End and parts of the Back Bay were built by developers who erected several rows of identical houses at one time. Thus, the ironwork on such row houses is usually of the same pattern, and the streets are architecturally unified. The heavy cast iron stair rails of 158–162 West Canton Street provide a good example. (FIG. 66) The acanthus leaf scroll railing is seen throughout the South End and parts of Beacon Hill as well. The massive fence and gate at 61 Mount Vernon Street on Beacon Hill are similar but employ the anthemion or Greek honeysuckle motif. (FIGS. 67a, b) The fence is supported on lotus bud posts, while the gate employs anthemions and, cleverly, lotus buds to attach the gate to the granite posts.

Boston fence patterns are numerous and varied. One rather common low wrought iron fence uses a scroll-heart motif along with an arrow or trident. (FIG. 68) Posts and arrows are capped by balls. Another variation of the 'heart' fence is seen at 315 Dartmouth Street. (FIG. 69) Of great simplicity but considerable design merit is the wrought iron fence at 34 Mount Vernon Street. (FIG. 70) Here the pattern is simply alternating twisted and wavy square bars, each capped with a ball.

Some of the most remarkable wrought iron workmanship in Boston is found at the Ames-Webster mansion at 306 Dartmouth Street in Back Bay. The house was built in 1872 and enlarged in 1882 by the architect John Sturgis, who probably designed the ironwork. The design bears no resemblance to any other Boston work and may have been executed in England, as was much of Sturgis's architectural decoration. The unusual heavy wrought

FIGURE 59

Galveston's Ashton Villa displays an extraordinarily complete and well-maintained collection of fanciful Victorian cast and wrought iron. The two-level veranda has pointed arches filled with acanthus leaf scrolls supported by pairs of slender posts with Corinthian capitals. Fence and gate posts, made by Wood and Perot and appearing as pattern number 511 in their catalog of 1860–1861, depict corn intertwined with morning glories, topped by sunflowers and a basket of fruit. The smaller pair of gate posts, topped by ears of corn, rest on pumpkins. The gates and fence do not match the 'corn' posts. However, Wood and Perot did make fencing and gates of this pattern. These can be seen at 1448 Prytania Street in New Orleans. (Galveston, Texas; Ashton Villa, 2328 Broadway; built by James Moreau Brown soon after 1853)

Regional Ironwork

A rather simple and characteristic Philadelphia railing design gains importance through repetition on each of several adjacent row houses. (273–279 Fourth Street, Philadelphia.)

A characteristic Philadelphia wrought iron pattern, simple but elegant, is found in this divided stair. (Philadelphia, 715 Spruce Street) (Photo by Michael Southworth)

FIGURE 62
Two Greek key borders frame rows of
x's with rosettes at each crossing in
this matching stair rail and fence fabricated largely of flat iron strips. This
design appears in Wood and Perot's
1858 catalog, design number 30. (Philadelphia, 708–710 Spruce Street)
(Photo by Michael Southworth)

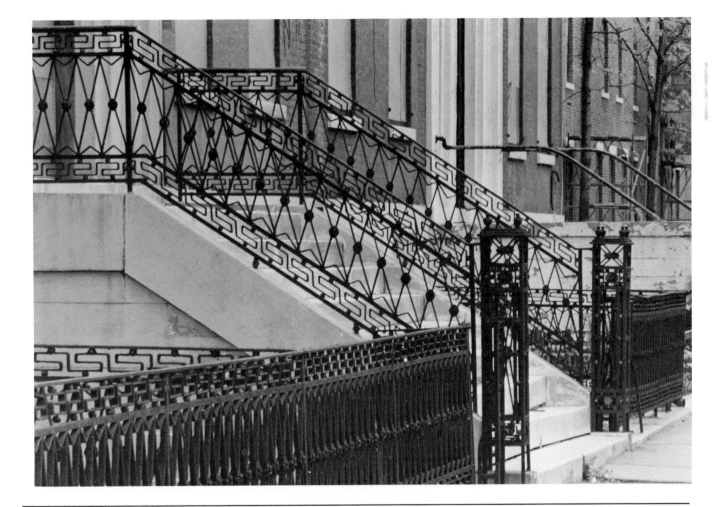

FIGURE 63

This fence design is uniquely Philadelphia. Some may feel the row of
cast seven-pointed stars an inappropriate cresting for the rather complicated fence of wrought scrollwork.
There would probably be no objection
to the stars as cresting if stars had
also been used in place of the floral
rosettes. (Philadelphia, 270 Third
Street) (Photo by Michael Southworth)

FIGURE 64

The ironwork here predates the architecture. This very unusual old
wrought iron gateway has been
installed on a contemporary house in
Society Hill. The basic panels are
composed of flat iron strips woven
together and riveted. Above this,
scrolls and twists rise to a dramatic
'V'-shaped framing of the gateway.
(Philadelphia, 433 Spruce Street)

FIGURE 65
*In this cast iron fence the popular
Greek revival motif, the anthemion, is
given an unusually heavy interpretation. Its weight, however, is consistent with the massive, temple-like
bank building. The strong black pattern of the ironwork is set off by the
white stone, making the fence the
most dominant decorative element.
(Philadelphia, Library Street; Second
Bank of the United States, 1824–1836,
later Philadelphia Custom House;
William Strickland, Architect) (Photo
by Michael Southworth)*

FIGURE 66

Developers of Boston's South End often built complete rows of houses at one time and installed matching stair rails on the entire row to create strong visual unity on the street. For this reason all original, developer-installed iron in the South End is cast. This group of three cast iron stair rails remains from a larger original group. The pattern was very popular and can be seen on several South End streets. It uses elaborate heavy acanthus scrolls cast in a closed mold. Because it is compact and low it serves as a stair edging rather than a hand rail. (Boston, 158–162 West Canton Street)

Ornamental Ironwork

This fine gate, largely of cast iron, uses the popular nineteenth-century motifs of anthemion and lotus. Supports for the gate in the form of vines and lotus buds are carefully designed to fit the carved granite posts. (Boston, 61 Mt. Vernon Street; built 1837)

Motifs seen in the gate at this address (Fig. 67a) are adapted for this massive and unusual cast iron fence. Lotus bud posts support large scroll vines with anthemion and lotus motifs. Elaborate patterns such as this benefit from simple surroundings. (Boston, 61 Mt. Vernon Street, built 1837)

FIGURE 68

The inverted heart/scroll motif is common in Boston's Back Bay. This is a particularly good example in a simple, low, wrought edging fence that could be reproduced today. Balls top all the verticals and a forged diamond pendant penetrates the heart. Notice the concern with the joint at the facade of the house where the scroll bracket climbs up the wall. (Boston, 115 Commonwealth Avenue; house built 1876, Cummings & Sears, Architects; fence probably executed by F. Krasser of Roxbury, Mass.)

FIGURE 69
Compare this inverted heart motif
fence with the one at 115 Commonwealth Avenue (Fig. 68). This is taller
and incorporates three horizontal
bands in the design. The scroll pairs
no longer line up vertically but rather
adjust to form new compositions at
each level. Note the pair of hammered
leaf motifs rising out of the heart in
the bottom band. (Boston, 315 Dartmouth Street; built 1870)

FIGURE 70
This amusing and simple wrought
iron fence uses only alternating
twisted and wavy square iron bars,
each topped with a ball. The pattern
could easily be reproduced today—
but would be disastrous in thin stock.
(Boston, 34 Mt. Vernon Street, built
1822)

Regional Ironwork

iron fence uses flower and vine themes, elaborately intertwined in three dimensions. (FIG. 71) Open spiral posts support and provide visual relief to the complex floral panels. Motifs from the fence reappear in iron wall sconces inside the great hall.

The wrought iron gate of this house, also important, is better preserved than the fence. (FIGS. 72a, b) Acanthus leaf scrollwork provides the theme for the design, with a series of dense, subdivided circles appearing at the bottom of the gates. Amusing gargoyles with long leaf-tipped tongues sit atop the latch rail and flow into the vinework. As the scrolls rise to the top, the ironwork becomes lighter, more open. The workmanship is superb, although the gates have been covered with an unfortunate layer of thick enamel paint that obscures the hand-wrought details.

One of Boston's outstanding cast iron patterns appears in Beacon Hill balconies at 75, 77, 79, and 83 Pinckney Street, at 59 Hancock Street, and on the Second and Third Harrison Grey Otis houses, both designed by Charles Bullfinch in the early nineteenth century (85 Mount Vernon Street and 45 Beacon Street, respectively). (FIG. 73) For cast iron, the pattern is unusually light and delicate; it actually looks like, and may in fact be a copy of, a piece first executed in wrought iron. Compared with the gates of St. Michael's Churchyard in Charleston (FIGS. 45a, b), as well as other southern examples, the design is austere, as might be expected in early nineteenth-century Boston. A diagonal interlaced band motif, sometimes called Chinese fretwork, fills panels that are separated by a vertical Greek key strip. Direct sunlight intensifies the ironwork and creates delightful shadows. The pattern provides interest but never overwhelms the architecture, making it an appropriate choice for the classic revival style. The simplicity of the pattern also recommends it for contemporary use.

Several fine cast iron balconies on Beacon Hill employ the anthemion motif. One is the handsome balcony at 91 Pinckney Street, in which fully bloomed anthemions or palmettes alternate with lotus blossoms. (FIG. 74) At 75 Hancock Street another interpretation of the same idea is seen. (FIG. 27) Both have simplicity, lightness, and harmony unusual for cast ironwork.

Wrought ironwork is an integral part of McKim, Mead, and White's monumental Boston Public Library, built 1888–1895.

FIGURE 71
This elaborate wrought iron fence of intertwined scrolls, leaves, and flowers is extremely three-dimensional, with events occurring in several different layers. Note the open coil posts. Iron wall sconces inside the house relate to the leaf theme in the fence. (Boston, Ames-Webster House, 306 Dartmouth Street; built 1872, enlarged 1882; John Sturgis, Architect)

Regional Ironwork

In this wonderful wrought iron gate, the pattern becomes increasingly light and open toward the top. Near the bottom we encounter strange beasts and leaves. (Boston, Ames-Webster House, 306 Dartmouth Street; built 1872, enlarged 1882; John Sturgis, Architect)

*These fantastic creatures stare fero-
ciously at each other through acanthus leaves, mouths wide open and
long serpent tongues hanging out,
lying across their backs and finally
terminating in a leaf. Their tails
merge with the scrollwork that forms
the rest of the gate. (Boston, Ames-
Webster House, 306 Dartmouth
Street; built 1872, enlarged 1882; John
Sturgis, Architect)*

Balconies of three houses in a row share what we call the 'Bulfinch pattern.' Though there is no definitive evidence that Bulfinch designed the pattern, it occurs on several buildings he designed and is extremely handsome on his architecture. Panels of 'interlaced' diagonal segments, sometimes called the Chinese fretwork pattern, alternate with Greek key bands. The simplicity of the pattern (minus Greek key) makes it equally appropriate for some modern architecture and has the advantage of relatively simple fabrication. (Boston, 75–79 Pinckney Street; nineteenth century)

Ornamental Ironwork

FIGURE 74
This handsome cast iron railing is one of the finest examples using the classical anthemion pattern, which consists of alternating palmettes and lotus blossoms linked with scroll vines. The pattern for this design appears in Asher Benjamin's Practice of Architecture *(1833). (Boston, 91 Pinckney Street; nineteenth century)*

FIGURE 75
Boston's Public Library contains a variety of distinguished ironwork, both outside and inside. The entry lanterns, surely the most dramatic pieces, exhibit superb workmanship. Inspired by Niccoto Grosso's lanterns for the Florentine Renaissance Palazzo Strozzi, these are more animated. Over the entries a flock of lanterns topped by spikes swoops down on long arms. (Boston, Public Library, Copley Square; 1888–1895, McKim, Mead, and White, Architects; ironwork manufactured by Snead & Co., Louisville, Ky.)

The architects designed handsome iron gates for each of several entrances, along with dramatic clusters of outdoor lanterns and an elaborate subway kiosk at Copley Station on the north side of the building. (FIG. 75) This superb work was hand wrought and forged in Louisville, Kentucky by Snead and Company. Inside, the wrought iron gates to the main reading room were made in Venice.

The Union Club at 8 Park Street on the Boston Common illustrates the artistic potential of fire escapes. (FIG. 76) At the second floor level, the fire escape is a cast iron veranda using the anthemion motif. The anthemion also appears on the cresting of the veranda roof. The fourth floor has a simple cast iron balcony with anthemion medallions at the supporting posts. On the fifth floor, the balcony is of wrought iron scrollwork supported by elongated scroll brackets. All balconies are connected vertically to the ground by means of wrought iron ladders, installed before modern requirements for fire stairways. Scrollwork on the ladder rungs and along the sides conceals the utilitarian nature of the ironwork; when the sun shines the ladders create lively shadows against the brick facade.

New York

Some of the first producers of architectural cast iron were in New York. One of the largest of these, Janes, Kirtland & Company, was established in 1845 on Fulton Street in lower Manhattan. Like many cast iron companies, it first manufactured practical items—cooking stoves and furnaces—but during the 1850's added ornamental ironwork to its line. Patterns such as the cast iron verandas on Gramercy Park and East 18 Street (FIG. 77) seem out of place in New York but were in fact first produced in New York and Boston foundries and shipped South before being taken over by southern foundries. Unfortunately, New York's dramatic transformation into a world business center meant the destruction of most of its early architectural ironwork except for scattered sites such as Gramercy Park, Washington Square, parts of Greenwich Village, Chelsea, the Upper East Side, Brooklyn Heights and Cobble Hill, and scattered banks and institutions. (FIGS. 77–79) On the other hand, much of New York's large collection of cast iron buildings remains intact and is well-documented elsewhere.

FIGURE 76

The elaborate ironwork on the Union Club illustrates the successful integration of a fire escape into the overall decoration of a building. Ladders at each end of the balconies are almost concealed in elaborate wrought iron scrollwork and create the effect of climbing greenery. Beautiful elongated scroll brackets support the top balcony. Cast iron anthemion cresting tops the second floor veranda. (Boston, Union Club, 8 Park Street)

FIGURE 77
This popular cast iron veranda pattern can be found in Savannah and elsewhere in the South. Joining two houses, the veranda has entrance porticoes defined by pilasters and anthemion cresting. Note the cast iron filigree risers of the stairway. (New York City, 326–330 East 18 Street) (Photo by Michael Southworth)

FIGURE 78
The ironwork of Washington Square, although of varied patterns, creates a harmony and richness that would otherwise be lacking. In the foreground fence the anthemion alternates with spears while a Greek key lines the bottom. Interestingly, the stair rail and balcony in the background are identical to some found in Savannah (See figure 119). (New York City, Washington Square North) (Photo by Gottscho-Schleisner, Inc.) from New York Landmarks by Alan Burnham.

FIGURE 79
Wrought iron lanterns, fences, and balcony railings are combined here. Except for the unrelated contemporary fence, the other pieces share the same scroll motif. Lanterns are supported on expansive scroll brackets. An unusual acanthus leaf overthrow on the balcony railing marks the entrance below. (New York City, 16 Gramercy Park) (Photo by George Gibson)

FIGURE 80
Richard Upjohn's cast iron fence for the Boston Common, melted for wartime armaments, was finally restored in 1976.

New York's wealth made possible numerous commissions to artists in wrought iron. Among these was Samuel Yellin whose ironwork in New York includes the J. P. Morgan Library gates, teller screens for the Chase National Bank, a gate for the Harkness Burial Garden at Woodlawn Cemetery, and many pieces for the Cloisters and elsewhere. (FIGS. 82, 95, 97)

Lost Ironwork

Although much pre-twentieth-century American ironwork still exists, an equal amount has been lost, much of it through demolition. Many prize pieces have turned up in scrap iron yards and a few survivors have made their way into antique shops. Fires, too, have destroyed much, particularly wrought iron, which is more susceptible to fire damage than cast iron. Still more architectural ironwork has been lost through neglect. Without regular maintenance, cast iron, being brittle and subject to rust, simply falls apart. In both Boston's Back Bay and South End we have observed the decay of several fine nineteenth-century cast iron fences.

Unfortunately, much architectural ironwork, both wrought and cast, has been donated or taken for scrap in several wars. In Charleston, wrought iron was melted down for horseshoes of the Continental forces. During the Civil War, sacrifices were made for the Ironclad, and, toward the end of the war, any iron not fixed in place was collected for the cause by squads of men.[15] In Boston, the ironwork of many private homes in Back Bay and Beacon Hill was sacrificed for various patriotic causes. Part of the Public Garden cast iron fence, installed in 1862, and much of the Common fence, designed by Richard Upjohn, were taken to be melted for armaments during World War II. It is said the latter was never used and was thrown into the Boston Harbor! Fortunately, both of these have recently been fully restored. (FIG. 80) But most of the Boston fences sacrificed for national defense still remain unreplaced, with cut iron stubs jutting out of the granite bases as mute reminders.

FIGURE 81
Samuel Yellin is shown in his studio with an elegant iron sewing box he made as a gift for one of his clients. Yellin's Philadelphia workshop contains an excellent museum of his work.

FIGURE 81b
Samuel Yellin at the forge, 1927.

NOTE: *Figures 81–98 courtesy of Samuel Yellin Metalworkers Co.*

Ornamental Ironwork

5 Twentieth-Century American Artists in Iron

Iron, one of the strongest of the metals, has been overlooked as a creative medium in modern times. Most artisans seem to prefer more precious metals—gold, silver, platinum, bronze, or copper. In ancient times, however, iron itself was considered a precious metal. The Sumerians called it 'the metal of heaven,' having first discovered it in meteorites thought to have been thrown to earth by gods. Even today we see evidence of this ancient belief in the magical powers of iron in the 'lucky horseshoe' tacked over doorways. Supernatural powers were attributed to ancient ironworkers because of their unique skills and the fiery drama of transforming the rock-like masses into works of art and utility. Some cultures considered the smith a kin of Satan. In Malabar, India, the smith was considered the lowliest of the untouchables, capable of polluting a Brahman at a distance of twenty-four feet. In contrast, some African tribal cultures elevated the smith to the high status of shaman or witchdoctor. Smithing was usually hereditary, passing from father to eldest son; ironworking techniques were kept secret and handed down through the family. Ostracized from society, the smith was often of a different race than his countrymen.[16] Today, at least in the Western world, the superstitions and social restrictions surrounding the smith have disappeared. As the nineteenth and twentieth centuries have rediscovered the value of hand crafts, the ironworker has achieved the status of respected artist.

Samuel Yellin

More than any other single American ironworker, Samuel Yellin established iron as an art form and may be considered America's counterpart to the great French art smith, Edgar Brandt. Yellin, born in Galicia, Poland in 1885, began apprenticing with a Russian smith at age seven; by the age of seventeen he had become a master craftsman. In 1906, he came to America, spending most of his career in Philadelphia, where he worked and taught. He was enormously successful. By 1920 his famed Arch Street Metal-workers Studio at 5520–24 Arch Street, built in 1910, employed over two hundred craftsmen. And after the day's work, his shop was open to all who wanted to learn his craft. The workshop, reminiscent of a medieval Spanish palace, is still operating today and has a large forge, an extensive library of books on metal work, Yellin's salon or studio, and a fine museum. Although Yellin died in 1940, his work survives in the museum that exhibits his numerous 'sketches in iron'—study pieces in wrought iron—as well as old European ironwork he collected.[17]

Yellin's work maintained an extraordinary level of craftsmanship and design ingenuity. His tools and methods were largely the same as those of much earlier centuries, but in addition to being master of all historic ironworking techniques—forging, fire weld-ing, twisting, fullering, flattening, punching, incising, splitting, repoussé—he made numerous contributions of his own. One of his favored joinery techniques avoided rigid weld connections; instead, iron units were loose-linked, strong yet flexible. (FIGS. 82, 83) Much of his work employs ingenious animal and floral motifs reminiscent of medieval European work, yet completely original. (FIGS. 84a, b) Other work is totally contemporary in feeling and demonstrates his mastery of pure form. (FIG. 85)

In creating ironwork, Yellin first made small pen sketches of his idea, then a 'sketch in iron,' a study section in which the concept was developed in the material itself. He then prepared full size architectural drawings for execution of the final work, leaving details for spontaneous execution on the anvil. To encourage spontaneity, creativity, and variation, Yellin never referred to the 'sketch in iron' in final execution. In Yellin's words, 'It is this actual study in the metal which gives the work its unexpected-ness and charm, and this can only come from a deep knowledge and love of the material.' [18] Yellin abhorred cast iron. It repre-sented dry repetition and uniformity; he worked only in wrought iron. Forging created the variety and spontaneity he considered essential to make the iron live. Yellin's views on early ironwork contain much of his own philosophy:

'The interest and charm which the most unpracticed observer must find in the work of the early craftsmen in iron is due to the fact that the metal was worked at a red or white heat. There was no time for measuring or copying a design save by the eye. Thus we get a spontaneity and a virility in forged work which expresses the life of the metal and gives the work its unexpected charm. These old craftsmen knew every branch of their work; they lavished as much skill and creative ability on a small handle as upon a great gate. No detail was overlooked, no matter how small or insignificant . . . The sincere nature of craftsmanship and the proper use of materials for ends to which they are well adapted is little understood today. This is not because there is any lack of information on the subject, but because the perfection of the mechanical means of production at our disposal has blinded many to the simplicity of the means which produced the great works of the past.' [19]

Yellin's work can be seen throughout the country, some of it at Harvard and Princeton Universities, the Washington Cathedral, the Detroit Institute of Arts and Public Library, the University of Pittsburgh, and the Cloisters in New York City.[20] (FIGS. 81–98)

Contemporary Smiths

Considering the quantity of ironwork being produced today in the United States, it is remarkable how little is of any real artistic interest or quality. A few scattered workers still treat iron as a creative medium, and there is some evidence of a renaissance of ironwork among metal artists. Today's artists generally use mild steel instead of the difficult-to-obtain wrought iron of the traditional smith. The repertoire of techniques has been expanded to include torch and arc welds and numerous power tools. Many contemporary smiths have come to iron from gold or silver smithing or from sculpture and they value iron for several reasons.[21]

RONALD PEARSON: '. . . The immediacy of forging iron brings together the work of the hand and the concepts of the mind.'

SVETOZAR RADAKOVICH: 'The almost primitive molding together of fire and iron and force is fascinating. But this primitive force can be brought to a peak of elegant power and delicacy . . . Even the simplest of forms take on a richness and strength they wouldn't have in another medium . . . The pleasure is as much in the process as in the result.'

JAMES HUBBELL: 'The simplicity and directness of the method is like being able to draw into the air . . .'

Twentieth-Century American Artists in Iron

STANLEY LECHTZIN: '... It is the immediate response of the hot iron under the hammer that I find so exhilarating. I am attempting to capture the feeling of a fluid arrested in motion, which is typical, yet so elusive, in the best wrought iron of the past.'

ALBERT PALEY: 'Wrought iron is more than a material; it is an attitude towards and an expression of metal. The inherent plasticity of metal, realized in the various cold working processes, is readily apparent in the hot working of ferrous metals. The rigid rod or plate seemingly returns to its plastic origin when heated to be controlled and guided. The complete diversity of approach and process is a stimulating counterpart to my involvement as a goldsmith.'

Albert Paley

Albert Paley, of Rochester, New York, considered one of the more significant contemporary metalsmiths, began his career as a goldsmith but is increasingly involved in large-scale architectural ironwork. For Paley, ironwork is an art form demanding all the creative energy of painting and sculpture. Traditional techniques and design motifs of the romantic village smithy do not constrain him. Rather, he suits techniques to his own artistic ends, drawing on the entire repertoire of methods and materials made available by modern technology. He intends, for instance, to explore the artistic potentials of Cor-Ten and stainless steel. Though he uses rough sketches in formulating a concept, intuitive response to the material is important to Paley. Each commission is a new and discrete artistic adventure. His unique 'liquid' treatment of steel gives it a feeling of arrested motion, as in his gates for the Renwick Museum in Washington, D.C. (FIG. 100) Paley wants to respond to the plastic quality of iron: 'When iron is heated, it becomes extremely plastic and, at yellow heat, it is similar to taffy—resistant but bending quite easily.' The gates, of mild steel with touches of brass and copper for color, display a rich vocabulary of inventive connections. The sinuous wavy and curling strips of iron create an organic feeling, although there is no representational intent in any of Paley's work.[22]

FIGURE 82

This wonderful bank teller's screen illustrates a type of flexible large-scale iron screening developed by Yellin. Rings are loose-linked as in chain mail and are joined by tri-spiked bands related to the spiked plant motif at the top of the screen. (Bank screen by Samuel Yellin, Chase National Bank, New York City; Trowbridge & Livingston, Architects)

Twentieth-Century American Artists in Iron

Loose-linked closed 'S' loops form this sketch in iron by Yellin. Welds, pins, collars, and other rigid connections are avoided.

Ornamental Ironwork

FIGURES 84a,b
Although these gates are basically a simple bar grid joined by rosettes, the overthrow contains imaginative animals and a variety of thistles and flowers. The handle of the gate is an exotic ram with scrolled twists for horns. (Wrought iron gates by Samuel Yellin, Seattle Art Museum, 1933)

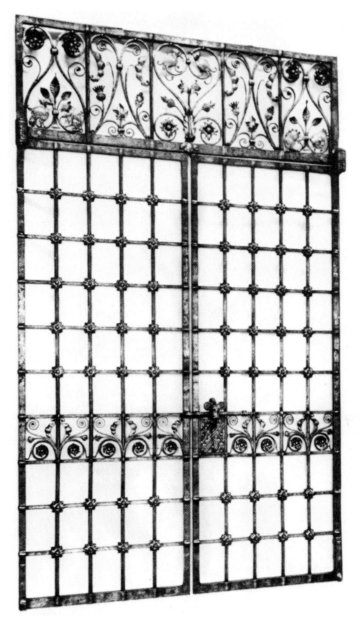

Twentieth-Century American Artists in Iron

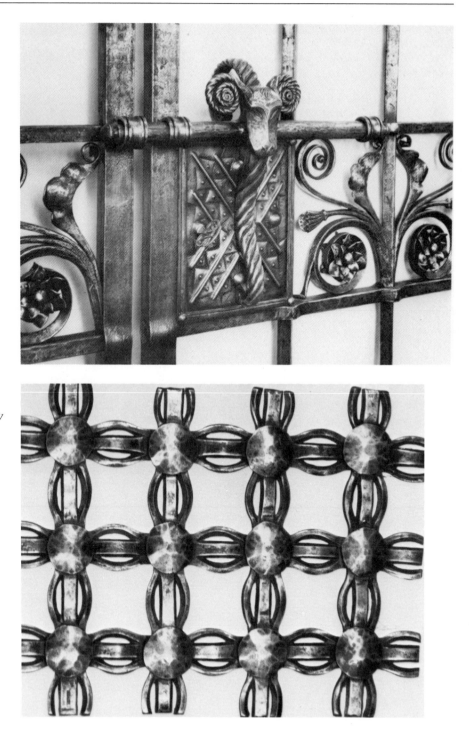

FIGURE 85
Any hint of traditional motifs is avoided in these totally contemporary 'sketches in iron' by Yellin.

Ornamental Ironwork

FIGURE 86
Split bars of iron intersect to create a grid pattern. (Iron study by Samuel Yellin)

FIGURE 87
Wavy bars with incised ribs have been notched to create hook-like scrolls. The ingenious pattern is particularly suitable for window or door grilles but is labor-intensive to produce. (Iron study by Samuel Yellin)

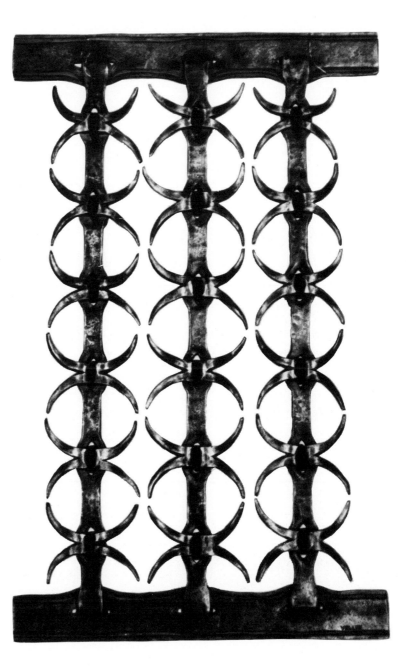

FIGURE 88
Study in iron by Samuel Yellin.

Ornamental Ironwork

FIGURE 89

FIGURE 90

Twisted double scrolls are banded together to form the infill for this grille
that Yellin made for a niche in his
office. The irregularities of hand
craftsmanship contribute to its
vitality.

The beauty of a natural unpainted
iron finish can be seen in this study in
iron by Samuel Yellin. Yellin avoided
painted finishes because they obscure
the natural character of wrought iron.
Many of Yellin's design motifs, such
as this one, were uniquely his and
were crafted in no other shop.

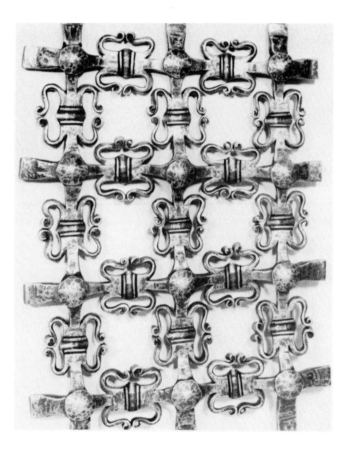

FIGURE 91

Unusual, irregular serpentine twists form the basic design. Other twists are used in the decorative overthrow and support posts. Note the double-petaled rosettes, wrought leaves, and lantern forms. Yellin consciously avoided machine-like repetition in his work; no two elements are identical. (Wrought iron gates by Samuel Yellin, The Citizens' Bank, Weston, West Virginia, 1929)

FIGURE 92

Yellin's designs for mundane radiator grilles illustrate his enormous creativity and attention to detail. Using the strict discipline of quadripartite scrolls and rosettes, he created rich variations, all in harmony with their architectural context. (Federal Reserve Bank, New York City, 1922)

Ornamental Ironwork

FIGURE 93
Here we see rather restrained gates of twisted bars with spiked flowers of elaborate three-dimensional tops. (Wrought iron gates by Samuel Yellin, Yale Gallery of Fine Arts, New Haven, Connecticut; Egerton Swartwout, Architect, 1928)

FIGURE 94
Reminiscent in their general style of much English ironwork, these large gates (over twenty-five feet tall) by Yellin use some original techniques and motifs. (Wrought iron gates by Samuel Yellin, McKinlock Memorial, Northwestern University, Chicago, Illinois; Childs & Smith, Architects, 1930)

Twentieth-Century American Artists in Iron

FIGURE 95
This pair of wrought iron gates is an unusual attempt to work in a highly pictorial manner with Chinese motifs including a pagoda lock. (L. J. Kolb residence, Philadelphia, 1926)

Ornamental Ironwork

FIGURE 96
Ornament in the form of leaves and rosettes is concentrated at the points where the bars intersect in this large and imposing set of gates fabricated of monel metal. (Yale Graduate School, New Haven, Connecticut, 1931)

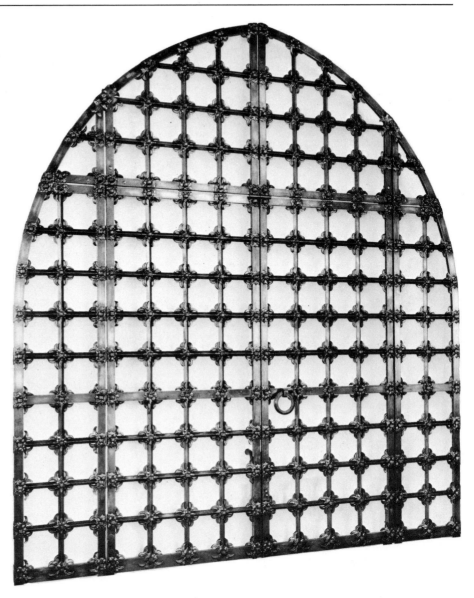

FIGURE 97
This intricate wrought iron screen is made up of repeated squares, each with an elaborate floral pattern that uses several different weights of iron, as well as varied motifs including scrolls, twists, flowers, birds, and leaves. (J. P. Morgan Library Annex, New York City, 1928)

FIGURE 98
The overthrow of these delightful
gates incorporates fanciful animals
and flowers in tree-like clusters. The
gates are filled with linked rings, each
filled with a quatrefoil, the loops of
which are joined by birds' heads.
(Wrought iron gates by Samuel Yellin,
Children's Chapel, Washington
Cathedral, Washington, D.C., 1934)

FIGURE 99
This fanciful wrought iron lizard gate is a completely delightful contemporary piece with every aspect of its functioning integrated into the composition. Its back is a solid mass of tight scrolls, and a wriggling serpent forms the left gate post. The eyes, legs, and feelers are extremely animated. The gray-brown natural oiled finish of the gate is particularly attractive, preserving all the details of hand craftsmanship. The house also has a 'sally port' gate in the form of a spider web.
(243 Delancey Street, Philadelphia; by Christopher T. Ray, Philadelphia)
(Photo by Michael Southworth)

FIGURE 100
These fine forged and fabricated steel gates by Albert Paley, though classical in their balanced composition, are not perfectly symmetrical. Paley treated the gates almost as large pieces of jewelry. As in his other work, ways of connecting elements are a constant source of fascination and invention. Polished bolts and washers are used as decorative elements. The gates also illustrate some exciting contemporary approaches to scrollwork. Copper and brass elements give the gates a wonderful color. (Renwick Gallery, Washington, D.C., 1974. 90¼ inches high, 72 inches wide, 1,200 pounds. Photo by Joseph Watson. © Paley Studio, Ltd.)

This gate by Albert Paley is a tour de force in techniques of iron connection. Verticals are composed of several tapered and intersecting forged steel bars joined together by collars. These intersect horizontal bars that in turn intersect the vertical side bars. (Gate #104, 3½ feet wide, 8½ feet high, 950 pounds, 1976. Photo by Bruce Miller. © Paley Studio, Ltd.)

This forged and fabricated steel fence varies in height from 6 feet to 13 feet over a length of 85 feet. This 32-foot-long section is one of three separate units comprising the massive 10,000-pound fence. Paley developed the schematic design for the fence in a pencil drawing. Some details were worked out by use of hose and flexible rods. Fabrication took sixteen months. (Hunter Museum of Art, Chattanooga, Tennessee, 1975. Photo by Joseph Watson. © Paley Studio, Ltd.)

Ornamental Ironwork

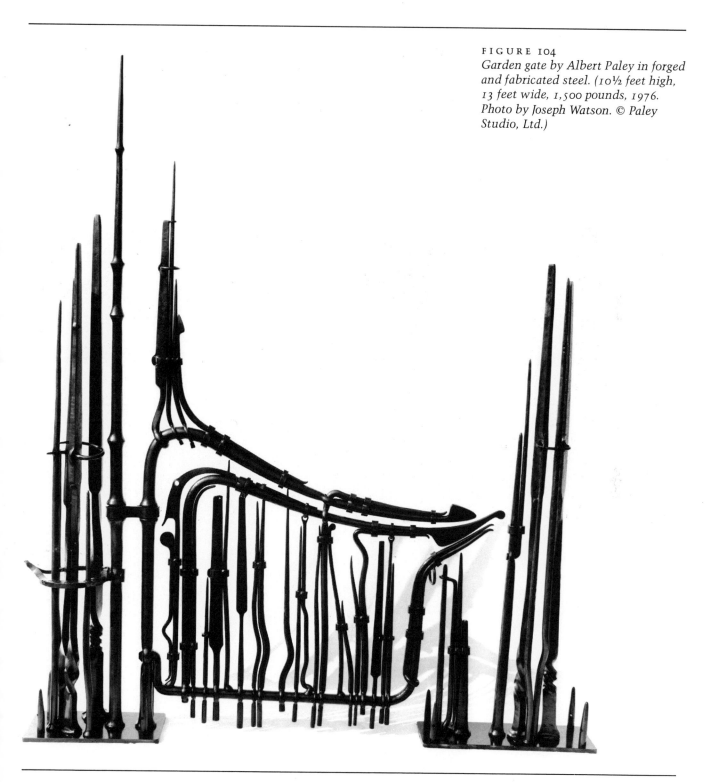

FIGURE 104
Garden gate by Albert Paley in forged and fabricated steel. (10½ feet high, 13 feet wide, 1,500 pounds, 1976. Photo by Joseph Watson. © Paley Studio, Ltd.)

Twentieth-Century American Artists in Iron

6

Portfolio: Fences, Gates, Stair Rails, Door and Window Grilles, Balconies, Verandas, Fire Escapes

FIGURE 105

Massive in cast iron, this fence is an excellent example of solid institutional dignity. The basic design motif is the round arch, inverted and capped with finials for the cresting. Note the same cresting used on the stair rail, *which helps unify the appearance of two different iron patterns in close juxtaposition. (Boston, Church of the Immaculate Conception, 761 Harrison Avenue; built 1861, P. C. Keeley, Architect)*

FIGURE 106

This relative of the spear fence tops the verticals with fleurs-de-lis alternating with knobs. Added to this is the extensive use of 'C' scrolls in an overall composition of three horizontal bands. The top band is the most ornate, but something very interesting is happening at the bottom. As the fence marches down the hill to the left, the upper three bands remain horizontal with respect to each other and the building behind, but the bottom of the fence follows the slope. This is an intriguing approach to hill locations. (Boston, 46 Beacon Street; Eben Jordan House)

FIGURE 107

An example of the alternating spear fence, this one adds short spikes to the bottom rail and simple scroll ornaments to the bottom of the top rail. The corner post is capped by a cast pineapple or acorn ornament. (Boston, 111 Commonwealth Avenue)

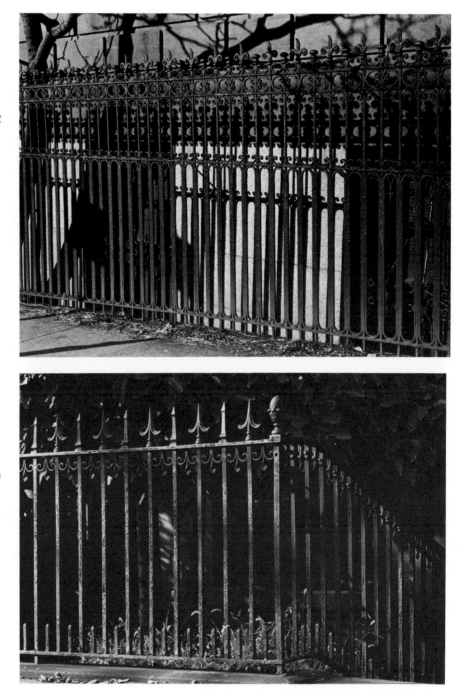

FIGURE 108
Appearing very flat and two-dimensional, this curious fence is actually made of unusually wide stock maintaining a minimum depth throughout of two and one-half inches. The concentric circles and cross are suspended by four intersecting spears. For a related example, see the crossed arrow motif suspended in the center of the New Orleans fence (Fig. 109). (Boston, 278 Clarendon Street)

FIGURE 109
This fence typifies the light approach of New Orleans ironwork. Bows tie together the suspended crossed arrows at the center. See Fig. 108 for a much heavier use of a suspended motif. (New Orleans, 415 Burgundy Street)

Ornamental Ironwork

FIGURE IIO

This cast iron fence is set into a stone curb and corner posts with no intermediary posts along the 15 foot length. For cast iron this is an unusually simple and austere composition. (Boston, 15 Commonwealth Avenue; house built 1867, Snell & Gregerson, Architects)

FIGURE III

A popular Victorian pattern seen in many American cities is illustrated in this cast iron balustrade. Fluted columns and the acanthus leaf are the basic motifs. (Boston, 137 Beacon Street; house built 1860, Edward Cabot, Architect)

FIGURE 112

This unusual wrought iron scroll pattern uses graduated scrolls of four different sizes, arranged around a central stalk. Alternating scroll clusters are inverted, with scrolls riveted to each other at contact points. The pattern is seen at several Commonwealth Avenue addresses including 207 Commonwealth, where it appears with an urn motif balustrade. (Boston, 207 and 213 Commonwealth Avenue; built 1883, Rotch & Tilden, Architects)

FIGURE 113
Elongated 'S' scrolls of strap iron provide ornament as well as diagonal bracing in a pattern that is simple enough to be fabricated today. Vertical bars, twisted and topped by forged tridents, discourage climbing. (Boston, 12 Fairfield Street; built 1879, Cabot & Chandler, Architects)

Portfolio

FIGURE 114

This unusual but simple and well-executed fence alternates sections of cyma-curved diagonals and straight iron bars. A pattern such as this could be imitated today with little difficulty. (Boston, 6 Joy Street; Lyman-Paine house until 1943; built 1824, Alexander Parris, Architect)

FIGURE 115

The streets of old Charleston are unique because of the fine wrought iron gates on most houses. Here, each pair of gates is different, yet harmonious. The scroll lyre and lattice patterns dominate the gates on the left, the top panel incorporating a lantern. The gates at the right are topped by a panel resembling a fan light, the gates themselves using purely geometric themes. (Charleston, S.C.; 133 Church Street)

Ornamental Ironwork

FIGURE 116

With strong defense, economic, and technical constraints, some visual amenity has definitely been introduced into this contemporary gate, although the workmanship is somewhat crude. The gates are fabricated from hollow square tubing. (Charleston, S.C.; 40 North Market Street)

FIGURE 117

The spear fence varies its height to form a swag, as do the spears in the gate. Scrolled post supports and open scroll cresting on the overthrow of the gate are characteristic of Charleston wrought iron. See Fig. 12 for a detail of the fine workmanship of this fence. (Charleston, S.C., Kahal Kadosh Beth Elohim Synagogue, 74 Hasell Street; 1838, C. L. Warner, Architect)

FIGURE 118
The graceful double stair is a southern tradition. Here the cast and wrought iron stair rail is continued (without the bottom border) across the front as a fence. (Savannah, Moses Eastman House, 17 West McDonough Street; built 1844, Charles B. Clusky)

FIGURE 119
Both stair rail and balcony use a simple but effective pattern of alternating cast iron ovals and straight verticals. The oval shape relates directly to the round arch over the main entrance, creating a very harmonious ensemble. (Savannah, 18 Harris Street)

FIGURE 120

This fine wrought iron stair rail is based on elaborate 'S'-pattern scrollwork. At the center of the landing a medallion is formed of rotating smaller scrolls. Scrolls also form supports for the entire railing and for the side braces on the landing. The termination at the bottom stair is treated handsomely with a reversal of the scroll under the hand rail. Note how the hand rail is supported on balls. (Charleston, S.C., Exchange and Custom House, 122 East Bay; built 1767–1772, Peter and John Horlbeck, Architects)

Ornamental Ironwork

FIGURE 121
The form of the arched stone entrance is repeated in the frame of this elegant wrought iron and glass door. The pattern is somewhat open, yet defensive. The more dense pattern around the lock is an appropriate safety measure. (Boston, 107 Beacon Street; built 1862)

Portfolio

FIGURE 122

This extraordinary wrought iron door guard repeats design motifs found on the rest of the facade. The iron cornucopias at the lower left and right of the door can also be seen in the carved stone panel over the door. The pair of iron heads in the top corners of the door frame, said to represent the original owners of the house, are repeated as stained glass profiles in the window above. Note the date, 'Anno Domini MCMX' (1910), incised in the iron above the door. The entire composition is unique, filled with special meanings. The mail slot was cleverly built into the door as a vertical element symmetrical with the knob and lock. (Boston, 115 Commonwealth Avenue; ironwork by F. Krasser & Co., Roxbury, Mass., 1910; building built 1876, Cummings & Sears, Architects)

Ornamental Ironwork

FIGURE 123
Boston has little Art Deco architectural ironwork, but this building has a door guard, canopy, and lanterns all in the Art Deco style. The relatively simple pattern of the wrought iron door guard employs straight and curved segments relating to motifs in the lantern, the stone door frame, and the canopy support. (Boston, 56 Commonwealth Avenue; built 1930, G. N. Jacobs, Architect)

FIGURE 124

These elegant but relatively simple wrought iron door guards are sufficiently defensive despite the fact that they stop short of the top of the glass area. The flattened spear heads and corkscrew tendrils are unusual elements. (Boston, 149 Beacon Street; built 1861)

FIGURE 125

The windows in these wood doors are protected by a hinged iron grille that may be opened with a key for cleaning the glass. Scrolls and flowers grow out of a small urn at the bottom of the panel. (Boston, 143 Beacon Street; built 1861)

FIGURE 126
Heavy bars of wrought iron—round, square, and rectangular—form this secure and imposing window guard. (Boston, 131 Commonwealth Avenue; built 1880, Carl Fehmer, Architect)

FIGURE 127
Thin twisted strips of iron can create attractive shadow patterns and highlights with a modest amount of labor. In this example, strips are riveted between twists, the ends being scrolled to form a decorative border. (Boston, 330 Dartmouth Street; built 1889, Blaikie & Blaikie, Architects)

FIGURE 128
Besides having a balcony from the Tuileries Palace, the John Andrew House has two other distinctive pieces of wrought ironwork. The massive window guards are countered by filigree balcony railings of twisted "C" scrolls. (Boston, 32 Hereford Street, built 1884, McKim, Mead, & White, Architects.)

FIGURE 129
Although traditional techniques and design motifs are used in these wrought iron window guards, the work is contemporary. (By Dr. Francis Whitaker, Carbondale, Colorado)

FIGURE 130

A simple pattern of interlaced bands (Chinese fretwork) is combined with the Greek key in this wrought iron balcony. The pattern is seen in the Second Harrison Gray Otis House also, and several other Beacon Hill locations. (Boston, Third Harrison Gray Otis House, 45 Beacon Street; built 1806, Charles Bulfinch, Architect)

FIGURE 131
This elaborate pre-revolutionary wrought iron balcony uses a number of motifs including the urn, intersecting circular segments, and several scroll varieties. On this simple pale building, the iron is dominant, with shadow patterns rich and varied most of the day. Note the scroll support brackets. (Charleston, S.C.; Confederate Home, 60 Broad Street; built in 1800 by Gilbert Chalmers; restored in 1887 after 1886 earthquake)

FIGURE 132
This delicate cast iron balustrade has the characteristic lacy southern feeling. (Savannah, Lachlan McIntosh House, 110 East Oglethorpe Avenue; built before 1783)

Ornamental Ironwork

FIGURE 133
(Savannah, Andrew Low House, now Georgia Society of Colonial Dames, 325 Abercorn Street; built ca. 1848, John S. Norris, Architect) (Photo by Michael Southworth)

FIGURE 134

One of the many wrought iron gates for which Charleston is noted, this has a riveted lattice pattern surmounted by round scroll and leaf medallions reminiscent of the St. Michael's Church communion rail. The medallion is repeated in a larger scale in the balcony above, supported on scroll brackets. (Charleston, S.C.; 66 South Battery)

FIGURE 135
Elongated 'S' scrolls alternate with plain verticals in this simple, light-weight balcony railing. (Charleston, S.C.; 60 Meeting Street)

FIGURE 136
The classical anthemion alternates with another scroll plant form in this cast iron balcony. Beveled faces of the scrolls create strong light and shadow patterns (Boston, 89 Pinckney Street)

FIGURE 137

The two-level veranda on this house uses one cast iron pattern for the posts and overhead horizontals, while the railing is of a different but not inconsistent pattern. Bays of the veranda are established by the window spacing. In front of the veranda is a wrought iron spear fence with cast spear heads and fence posts. (New Orleans, Leathers-Buck House, 2027 Carondolet Street; built 1859, Henry Thiberge, Architect)

FIGURE 138

This wooden veranda probably had a wooden railing originally. With Greek revival architecture a complex iron pattern would have been absurd. The interlocked circular segments form a dignified pattern, but a less complicated composition might have been more effective on this handsome house. (Charleston, S.C., Branford-Horry House, 59 Meeting Street; built 1751–1767; veranda added in 1830)

FIGURE 139

This is an outstanding example of the proper way to add a fire balcony to bowfront buildings. The balcony follows the bow forms and enhances them. A simple but attractive design of cast iron segments was selected, and the scroll support brackets were chosen for their decorative as well as structural capacities. The result is a very pleasing addition to the facade that ornaments rather than detracts from the building's appearance. (Boston, 63–64 Beacon Street; built 1824, Ephraim Marsh, Architect)

7

Design: Visual Considerations

Pattern and Form

Patterns selected for ironwork ideally harmonize with both the architecture and with neighborhood iron styles. Patterns need not be complex or elaborate to be effective; some of the best are the simplest—for example, Boston's 'Bulfinch' grille (F I G. 73) or the simple scrollwork balcony in Charleston, S.C., at 60 Meeting Street (F I G. 135). Extreme complexity in ironwork requires just the right setting to work successfully. Simple but elegant patterns have wider application and are certainly easier to fabricate today.

Within the context of a single building facade, ironwork can be used to enhance the architecture. Iron cresting, for instance, is an effective Victorian device for highlighting bay windows or rooflines. (F I G. 2) With the addition of a balcony or veranda, a flat facade can be given three-dimensional interest. Balcony forms can highlight windows and create a rhythmic unifying theme, or, following the curves of bow-fronted buildings, they can effectively emphasize the form of the facade. (F I G S. 139, 140)

Ornament

The relationship between ironwork and the architecture it adorns is crucial. The basic form of the architectural style should be mirrored, and any decorative additions should relate to the established vocabulary of the building. This does not imply that slavish copies of period pieces are necessary on older buildings. Contemporary designs in iron can work well on old architecture if they are designed to harmonize with specific stylistic aspects. (F I G. 141) For example, ironwork can pick up a detail from the cornice, window lintels, or door ornament and use it as a basis for a pattern. And it is far better to do a good modern pattern than a poor imitation of an antique one. In a flamboyant Victorian neighborhood, the design of ironwork for a restrained neoclassic facade is a problem. 'Gingerbread' ornamentation would look absurd on the building. If the architecture is very restrained, with no curving motifs anywhere, then curves may not be appropriate for the ironwork; angular geometric patterns may be more desirable. If a more ornamental feeling is needed, curved motifs are probably most effective. And when several pieces of iron are used on one building—fence, window and door guards, balconies—they should relate in design, although they need not be identical. (FIGS. 142, 143)

Ironwork can also express the interests and personality of the owner. A horse enthusiast may want to install a hitching post—authentic or reproduction—in front of his house. (FIG. 144) The sailor may use nautical motifs; a gardener, some favorite flowers as the theme for ironwork. Or there is the possibility of using one's initials for decorative motifs, as has been done in Charleston and New Orleans. (FIG. 42)

Cast and wrought iron ornaments are difficult to integrate in a single piece. The heavy molded appearance of cast iron is quite out of character with the lighter bent and hammered appearance of wrought iron, except in small cast components—rosettes, finials, or balls. Unfortunately, the common cast iron grape vine is frequently seen mixed with twisted bars or scrolls. Beware—to combine these is to commit esthetic suicide. One might better have a chainlink fence and at least be honest about it!

The problem with cast iron is that even if a basic unit design is good, elements can be misapplied or used in grotesque combinations by an insensitive worker. Some cast components readily available today just can't help looking cheap—they are too thin and stereotyped. One can only hope that outstanding cast iron patterns of the past, such as Asher Benjamin's anthemion railing design, will again be made available. (FIG. 27) Several foundries, mainly in the South, cast traditional Victorian fences and balconies, as well as components such as balls, finials, and rosettes. These can be attractive combined with work of traditional design; they can also be dreadful.

Successful ornament is still possible despite the glut of unattractive decorative pieces. A number of quite acceptable ornaments can be fabricated at reasonable cost. Solid rings can be quickly sliced from iron pipe and incorporated into simple basic ironwork. (FIG. 145) Iron bars may be looped and curved around a standard form to produce repetitive curves, as along the top of a

FIGURE 140

These cast iron balconies supported
on fluted brackets highlight the fenestration pattern of the facade and
appear to have been designed
expressly for the house. The pattern
uses the inverted heart/scroll motif
with a row of leaves rimming the top.
(Charleston, S.C.; Louis de Saussure
House, 1 East Battery; built 1850–
1860)

FIGURE 141
This modern fence was designed for
Victorian Boston houses and uses
simple modern techniques available
to nearly any ironworker. A visual
rhythm is established by the alternating spacing of verticals. (Boston, 197
West Canton Street; fabricated by
Boston Design Corporation, 1975;
adapted from a window grille design
by the authors)

FIGURE 142
Several forms of heavy wrought iron-work appear on this 'French Renaissance' building—on the fence, gates, front door, and three balcony railings on the third floor. The ironwork was conceived as part of the total architectural design; it uses coordinated design motifs based on the scroll. (Boston, 130 Commonwealth Avenue; built 1882, Peabody & Stearns, Architects; facade remodeled 1905)

Ornamental Ironwork

FIGURE 143
A cast iron fence, balcony, and stair rail are combined in this characteristic South End bow front. The fence pattern is found in many 19th century catalogs and is almost identical to the one at 124 McDonough Street in Savannah. (Boston, 43 Union Square.)

FIGURE 144
This bird-like hitching post has lost its function but is a delightful nineteenth-century cast iron street ornament. (Boston, 33 Chestnut Street)

FIGURE 145

This very straightforward spear fence separating two row houses uses only one spear style alternating with shorter plain vertical bars. Notice that the plain verticals are shorter on both the top and bottom until the fence climbs the stairs. The only other decorative device is the row of circles at top and bottom of this six-foot-high fence. Note the door grille. (Boston, 57 Commonwealth Avenue; built 1874, Carl Fehmer, Architect)

Ornamental Ironwork

Stock

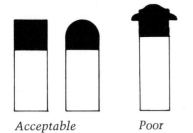

Acceptable   *Poor*

Twists

fence. (FIG. 141) A number of simple decorative devices are illustrated in detail in Chapter 9. An enterprising manufacturer should develop assorted interchangeable cast iron and mild steel components suited to contemporary tastes and do-it-yourself assembly; components could be designed for varied applications, from fences and window guards to outdoor furniture.

Square cross section iron is almost universal now, but round bars can also be attractively used. These are particularly suited to bent work such as the Savannah 'woven wire' patterns. (FIG. 146) Wide flat iron bars can create lovely ribbon-like effects with strong shadows and highlights. (FIG. 147) Don't feel limited to only one size or shape of stock within a single piece of ironwork. On the contrary, several sizes of iron stock can be used in one pattern with each lending interest to the design. The shape of the top rail capping a fence or balustrade should relate to the overall pattern and stock used. In nearly any case the popular compound-curved top rail iron strips are a poor choice. With square straight bars, a simple half-circle, square, or rectangular cross section would be more appropriate.

Weight is an important factor in design. Heavy iron normally has more visual presence than its lighter relatives. The exception is thin wide bars that often have greater visual power than their weight suggests. Another point is that heavy stock (more than $5/8$ inch square) can make a success of simple patterns that otherwise look flimsy.

One ubiquitous example of a poorly handled decorative device is the modern twist. Twists today are usually too thin and too widely spaced to be effective. (FIG. 148a) To create a strong pattern, bars should be twisted perhaps two to three revolutions, depending upon length. The older iron twists often used heavy stock that was one inch or more on a side. The result is impressive; there is a definite sense of power in that enormous twisted bar with the deep furrows on all sides. (FIG. 148b)

The modern interpretation of this simple and useful pattern could most generously be termed spaghetti in its visual impact. The stock is too thin, and the twists are barely apparent at a distance of more than five feet; the predominant effect is that of a mis-shapen iron rod. The one exception is the use of thin flat strips of

Design: Visual Considerations

FIGURE 146
In the 19th century, many companies
produced ornamental "woven wire"
window guards and fencing, the Victorian equivalent of chainlink fencing.
This example appeared in the 1894
catalog of Winslow Brothers Company, Chicago.

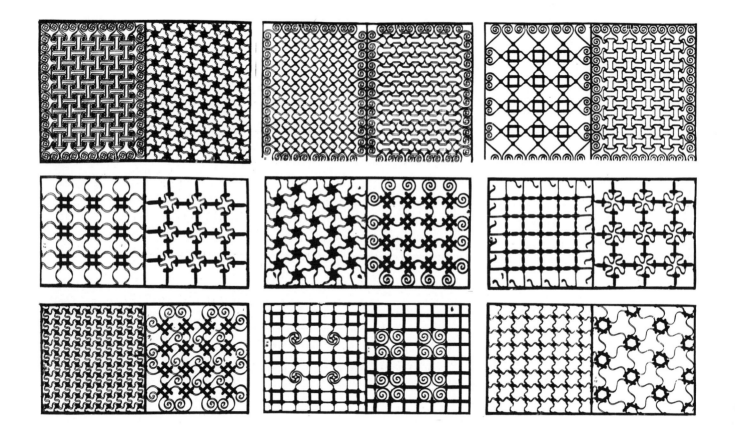

FIGURE 147
An elaborate scroll composition in a plain frame, this fence is entirely of wide, flat iron stock. Contrasts of light and shadow are dramatized by the thin, flat, ribbon-like bands of iron. The scroll pattern is relatively simple and could easily be duplicated today. (Boston, 161 Warren Avenue)

Design: Visual Considerations

FIGURE 148a
Flimsy twists mar much contemporary ironwork and should be avoided.

FIGURE 148b
Massive stock and closely spaced twists usually improve the esthetic value of the twist.

FIGURE 149
Twisted, ribbon-like strips of iron were a simple and economical way to ornament this utilitarian fire escape. (Boston, 108 Myrtle Street)

Ornamental Ironwork

iron, which, although lightweight and weak, create a rich form when twisted and closely spaced. (F I G. 149)

Old European work sometimes made use of compound twists in which two or more pieces of iron stock were twisted together. At times these were of two different cross sections—square and round, for example—creating rich rope effects. Such twists can be used effectively today to make contemporary patterns or to blend with Victorian and other period architecture. (F I G. 150)

Special Design Problems

Window Grilles

Ironwork should be designed to look attractive from both inside and outside the building. If well conceived, a window grille can have the effect of leaded glass or Gothic tracery, not prison bars. It will filter light, frame a view, or screen an unpleasant sight. For economy's sake, straight bars of iron are often used in today's window or door grilles to form the basic structure into which the decoration is incorporated. (F I G. 153)

Surprisingly, bar patterns often bear no relation to the pattern of window or door muntins. Given a four-over-four or six-over-six window muntin pattern, it would seem obvious that one could all but make the bars disappear from inside by placing them carefully and leaving only the decorative motifs visible against the view. Not so; bars are frequently placed at awkward intervals, completely ignoring the muntins and creating a hodge-podge from both outside and in. (F I G S. 151a, b)

With the standard double-hung window, any horizontal bar of the grille belongs in a position coincidental with the meeting rail. But the central decorative motif does not belong there; it would be completely obscured for viewers inside. A Victorian door with a large oval pane of glass should not have a rigid square pattern in its iron grille. The ironwork pattern should recognize in some manner its curved frame, though the exclusive use of curved members is by no means necessary.

The view *through* a window must also share primary emphasis in the design. If an important or favorite visual element falls in the center of the window, the major embellishment should probably not occur in the center but rather on the sides or top and bottom away from the point of greatest interest. Similarly, if the vista is pleasing except for a single unsightly element, heavy embellishment can mask the offending object. A fine view can be rein-

FIGURE 150 *(left)*
Rich twist patterns can be created by twisting two bars together.

FIGURE 152
Grille patterns can frame or obliterate views to the outside.

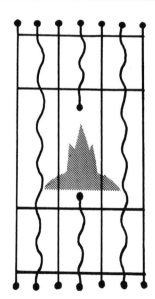

FIGURE 151a *(left)*
Bar patterns frequently bear no relation to the pattern of window or door muntins, creating a hodge-podge.

FIGURE 151b
Bars should relate to the module established by window and door muntins.

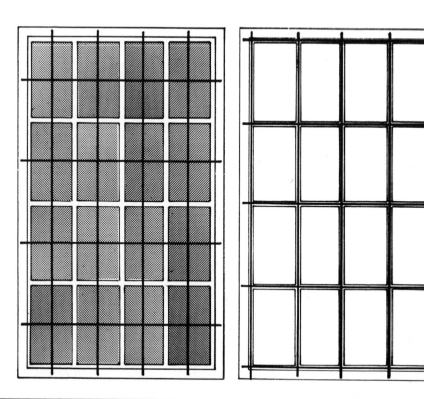

FIGURE 153

This wonderful contemporary window guard is just as secure as more traditional bar patterns but is also an exciting work of art. The freely formed rings break the monotonous bar pattern and create many small viewing frames. Iron bars were split to form the circles; bars were riveted together where the circles touch. (By Ivan Bailey Metal Studio, Atlanta, Georgia, 1972)

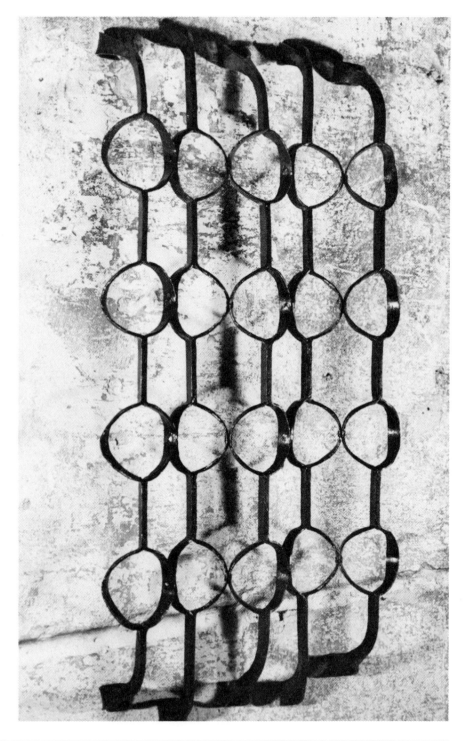

Design: Visual Considerations

forced and framed by the window grille pattern just as a bad one can be selectively blocked. (FIG. 152)

Air Conditioners

One of the most obtrusive problems in historic neighborhoods is the window air conditioner. Although proscribed by most architectural standards except for rear exposures, air conditioners nevertheless abound in the city. Iron box grilles projecting from the facade can be built to accommodate them, prevent theft, and camouflage them. (FIGS. 154, 155) A somewhat dense or elaborate pattern is called for if the camouflage attempt is to succeed. Painting the exterior of the air conditioner flat black, dark brown, or charcoal before installing it behind the ironwork also helps. For cooling efficiency, the top should be left a light color to reflect sunlight. On an upper floor where a window grille is not needed for security, iron balconies or low window guards can achieve the same effect.

Fire Escapes

Poorly designed ironwork can also ruin a building and may well lower property values. Too often this is what happens when fire escapes are added to residential buildings converted to apartments. (FIG. 156) Disastrous fire escape installations have occurred on bow front buildings in which the fire escape actually visually flattened the facade and camouflaged the bow. In other cases fire escapes cut across windows, creating havoc with fenestration patterns and permanently scarring inside views. In designing a fire escape, it is necessary to consider not only the design of the railings, but also steps, landings, and supporting brackets or posts. These are often as visible as the railing. (FIGS. 157, 158)

Ironwork and Plants

Historic ironwork has often used plant motifs as its decorative theme; indeed, some iron creates a sense of vegetation even though nothing organic is remotely present. Much southern ironwork contains local floral motifs such as the trailing vine and the passionflower. But iron has an even simpler relationship with vegetation. It can provide a framework for vines, flowers, ivy, or climbing plants such as wisteria, climbing roses, clematis, and morning glories. Ironwork balconies and window boxes can be used to provide a secure place for outdoor potted plants or portable window boxes. (FIG. 159) Window grilles can incorporate hooks for hanging plants, box areas for groups of plants, or rings to hold pots. (FIG. 160) Vegetation can be used to soften the con-

FIGURE 154

FIGURE 155

FIGURE 156

Box-style window guards, though not appropriate for all architecture, can perform more than a single function. They facilitate window washing, and they provide room for a planter or air conditioner. This wrought iron box guard is mounted on a very plain stucco facade. Decoration is of thin pressed or cast iron garlands, a central group of figures, urns, and rosettes. The hand-wrought markings are visible on this piece. (Boston, 109 Chestnut Street, built 1832)

Window guards may be designed to accommodate air conditioners.

By ignoring the architectural context, this fire escape has ruined the appearance of several row houses.

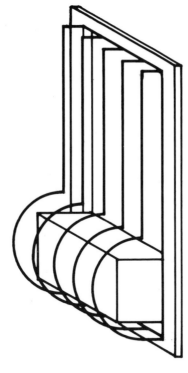

Design: Visual Considerations

FIGURE 157
The landings of this fire escape have
been designed to serve as balconies.
While the railings and circular
stairway have received design
attention, the platforms and supports
are rather unfortunate in this context.
(Boston, 3 Spruce Street)

FIGURE 158

This is a good illustration of how the typical ugly fire escape can be modified. The fire balconies follow carefully along the bows of the facade. It must be pointed out that this is a rear facade of a building, not the front. Decorative cast elements were added to the railing. Note the lions with fish-like tails. More design attention would be required for fire balconies on the front of a building, particularly with respect to the supporting brackets and floor grid. Nevertheless, this makes a presentable back view in contrast to the miserable appearance of most iron fire escapes. (Boston, 20 Mt. Vernon Street)

Design: Visual Considerations

FIGURE 159

Ironwork and flowers combine to make a pretty domestic setting. Even though motifs in the balcony and fence do not relate, the effect is still pleasing. The cast iron newel posts of the fence combine the Greek key and anthemion motifs while the simple square bars of the fence are topped by cast iron fleurs-de-lis. The balcony uses an alternating pattern of anthemion, lotus bud, and an unusual star-in-circle. (Boston, 23 Chestnut Street; built 1809, Jeremiah Gardner, Architect)

FIGURE 160
An unusual wrought iron arch screen not only defines the dividing line between the public street and private house, but also serves as a plant and lantern holder. (Boston, 21 West Cedar Street)

nection between the ground, iron, and architecture. Ivy, for example, can provide a beautiful transition from ironwork to ground. (FIG. 164)

Sun, Rain, Snow, and Ironwork

One of the pleasures of living with ironwork is to witness its interaction with sun, rain, and snow. The elements reveal different aspects of iron architecture, highlighting patterns and forms. In climates that have snow, ironwork can be designed to retain it, making black and white winter patterns. The iron window grille that can hold snowflakes before the window makes a delightful ornament. (FIG. 161)

After a rainstorm when the sun bursts out, black ironwork glistens. On wet iron, blacks are more intense, reflections are brighter; patterns are dazzling. Suddenly this reticent art form jumps out, demands attention, and proudly proclaims itself refreshed. Indoors on a rainy day, ornamental window guards frame wet and blurry pictures—miniatures of the rainy landscape. In a heavy thunderstorm when there's nothing beyond the window to be seen, the ironwork figures are a reassuring presence seen through prisms of drops and streams of rain on glass. The grille has a softness then, its distinct forms almost impressionistic.

In living with and looking at ironwork, one soon realizes that the *shadow patterns* cast by the iron fence, fire escape, or door guard often assume as much visual prominence as the iron piece itself. The multiple and ever-changing shadow patterns of the ironwork are the living esthetic of what is at first impression a static art form. (FIG. 162) The impact of iron's shadow should have consideration in design because it plays such an important role in our visual experience. During the day, the shadow patterns are alive, shifting from sunrise to sunset. While buildings are solid and immobile, the ironwork dances blithely, traversing a different path each season, moving day by day closer to the edge of the entry rug or the flower bed. Even at night shadow patterns are active and alive in the back-lighting of a door guard or window grille, or in fence shadows thrown from the street lamp. The iron window guard provides a filigree tracery against interior lighting. From outside it may be the only expression of a home, immediately establishing a personality for the visitor and passerby.

FIGURE 161
In snow, ironwork is intensified. Patterns catch soft mounds of snow to form striking contrasts with the hard black iron. (Boston, Back Bay) (Photo by Michael Southworth)

Design: Visual Considerations

FIGURE 162
The shadow effects are almost as important as the ironwork in this balcony. The delicate pattern of railing and floor grid are overlaid in the rich shadows that sharpen the bowfront. Note the fine simple scroll bracket supporting the balcony. The pattern is also seen at 63–64 Beacon Street. (Boston, 21 Chestnut Street; nineteenth century)

Ornamental Ironwork

The Architectural and Neighborhood Context

Architectural ironwork creates continuity along streets with otherwise disparate architecture. A typical American city street may have houses ranging from middle or late Victorian through the functional modern styles. Appropriate iron fences lining the front garden edges can unify divergent styles into a cohesive, attractive neighborhood. Repetitive balconies or stair railings can be used to create the same effect, although the greater the architectural differences in detailing, materials, or fenestration, the less successful will be treatment directly on the facade. The same stair balustrade repeated on each of a series of row houses can extend the importance of each unit to a larger and more imposing scale.

Height variation in facades is not a particular problem on a narrow street; balconies will work equally well in unifying streets with houses of similar or widely varying heights from three to six stories. From the ground, their height variations are hardly noticed on narrow streets. A row of houses of different periods but the same materials can also be unified by means of facade ironwork. However, on streets with diverse materials, from clapboard and brick to stone and glass, ironwork that moves away from the facade, such as stair railings or garden fences, will be more effective in unification. If houses stand directly on the sidewalk with no front garden or stair, iron lamp posts along the curb can create a sense of adjacent harmony, particularly if echoed by matching building-mounted iron fixtures hanging over the sidewalk at each doorway. These need not be of Colonial or Victorian design; a number of fine iron lanterns of contemporary design could be used.

On the other hand, when the architecture on a street is monotonously repetitive, ironwork can establish an individuality for otherwise anonymous buildings. In many parts of Savannah, Charleston, Boston, New York, and Philadelphia, ironwork provides a greater variety than architecture. Row house neighborhoods of even simple design can achieve individuality and interest through the creative use of ironwork patterns and forms. Of course the ironwork must be executed with restraint; gargantuan displays with no relation to each other or to the character of the neighborhood look absurd. And even to achieve an individual effect for each house, some basic structure must be maintained for the street. Neighbors might vary the pattern and bulk of ironwork but maintain the height, or they might vary height and pat-

Design: Visual Considerations

FIGURE 163
Stair rails create a rhythmic pattern on this hilly brick sidewalk, enhancing the whole street scene. The foreground rail and balcony both use the same pattern of simple 'C' scrolls, reminiscent of Philadelphia work. Although the pattern is effective, lightweight stock such as this is easily deformed accidentally, as this example shows. Note how foot scrapers are integrated into the stair rails. (Boston, Chestnut Street)

FIGURE 164
This dignified wrought iron spear fence is a good example of the 'step down' or bridge between fences of different heights. Without such a gesture to the height variations, a jarring effect could result. The lush ivy ground cover creates a soft transition between fence and ground. (Boston, 39–40 Beacon Street; house built in 1820, Alexander Parris, Architect)

Design: Visual Considerations

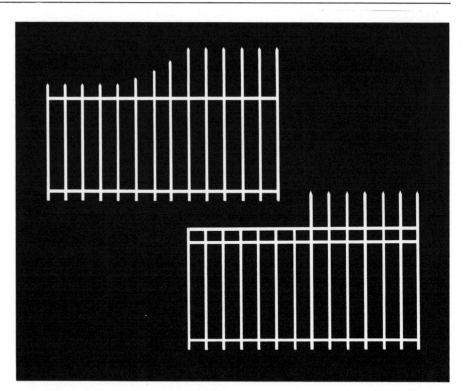

tern but maintain bulk and mass. Another approach to harmonious variation would be to use ironwork of the same pattern for differing applications. Some could use balconies and stair rails, while others might install window guards, over-door lanterns, door guards, or fencing, each element based on the same design.

It is particularly important to consider the effects of new ironwork on immediately adjacent neighbors. A new fence between existing iron fences must be planned with attention to height. Very convincing reasons are needed for varying height in such situations; too many different fence heights create visual chaos. Variations of less than a foot are usually not a problem unless there is a strong commitment along several lots to one height. If it is absolutely necessary to make drastic steps up or down, the discontinuity should be handled through a transitional element. (F I G. 164) For continuity, it is helpful to extend motifs or basic structural lines, such as the top rail, in the deviating fence. (F I G. 165)

8

Design: Practical Considerations

Design is sometimes considered to be the residual fluff left over after all practical necessities have been satisfied. In fact, the reverse is closer to the truth. Design is, rather, intelligent problem solving; it strives toward serviceable results in *all* areas of performance—one of them being the esthetic. In dealing with ironwork, the designer is concerned not only with visual considerations but also with solving problems of privacy, utility, and security. All of them are interconnected.

Defense

Doors and Windows

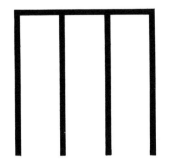

FIGURE 166
For security, bars in window or door guards should be no farther apart than 6″ on center.

As an element of architecture, ironwork has long connoted security and strength. An understanding of defense factors is essential in designing door and window grilles. Patterns must be tight enough to prevent intruders from climbing through if the glass is broken. Six inches on center between bars is the largest secure spacing for any pattern of parallel bars. Minimum head dimensions govern, since on a child or slender adult all other parts of the body could squeeze between the bars. (FIG. 166) The size and shape of iron stock must be determined by the job it is intended to do. Since window and door grilles are intended to serve a defensive function, they must be strong enough to resist easy bending or cutting; in dimensions, ½ inch by ½ inch is minimum for a square iron bar. For round stock, the minimum diameter is ⅝ inch. Stock heavier than these minimums provides additional security; lighter stock provides security, although it may be only a symbolic deterrent to intruders. Bars ½ inch by ½ inch should be connected laterally at least every 4 feet. One popular type of defensive window grille, unfortunately, is a woven wire mesh resembling chainlink fencing. It may be inexpensive, but it looks like a chicken coop on the inside and out and ruins any building to which it is attached. Moreover, it is weak and can be easily cut with wire cutters.

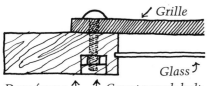

Grille ↙

Door frame ↗   ↖ Countersunk bolt

Glass ↗

FIGURE 167
Detail: Attaching grilles to wood doors.

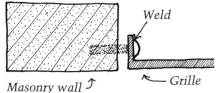

Weld

Masonry wall ↗   ↖ Grille

FIGURE 168
Detail: Attaching window grilles to masonry walls.

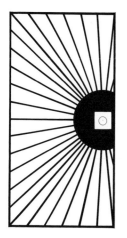

FIGURE 169
A dense filigree pattern protects the lock area of a gate.

Gates

Grilles made of appropriate material and pattern must then be installed securely, attached to the building so they cannot be removed from the outside. It follows that the connections must be as strong as the ironwork itself. If bolts are used on door grilles, they should have a plain head with the nut on the inside. (FIG. 167) These can be countersunk in the door and filled so they will not be visible inside. One-way headed screws may also be used. For installation of window grilles in masonry, one very secure and visually acceptable connection is shown. (FIG. 168) Short legs are welded perpendicular to the plane of the grille. Bolts or pins are inserted through these legs into the masonry. The heads are then welded onto the legs to prevent removal.

Glass paneled doors with iron grilles need special treatment. They should be keyed on both sides with a dead bolt for maximum security, or burglars could break the glass and reach inside to open the lock. Keying a lock on both sides is normally not permissible for fire exits in multiple-occupancy buildings, but sometimes variances are granted if a key is kept near the lock at all times. A dense filigree pattern or large plate around the lock area of the grille can reduce the possibility of a burglar reaching through the broken glass to turn the bolt. Push-button release locks for window guards are also available. These allow immediate release of the locking mechanism from the inside; the push button itself, however, must still be protected against operation from the outside.

Grilles need not be hinged for window cleaning if the grille is designed and mounted so as to leave enough space for washing. If the grille is hinged, a lock must be provided integral with the grille that can be opened only with a key, preferably from the inside. Rusting and icing problems with exterior grille locks are common and locks should be weather protected. Padlocks are unsightly and not very secure. It is best to avoid hinged and locked grilles. A better solution is to install a removable or hinged glass panel and leave the grille in place.

Iron gates are used variously at sally port entrances, on outdoor vestibules, and at entrances into gardens, driveways, and courtyards. For security, the gate must be keyed on both sides, or else the turn knob must be protected from the outside by a large plate or box or by an overall filigree pattern. The configuration must minimize the possibility that intruders could reach through and open the gate. (FIG. 169) Gates should be sufficiently high to keep intruders from climbing over the top.

Fences

The primary security function of fences is keeping pets and children in and intruders out. To be effective, the ironwork pattern of a fence should be closely spaced—4 inches to 6 inches maximum. Height should be sufficient to deter climbing, which means six feet or more for real security. Of course, fences much lower will be effective for child and pet control. The design of the fence should not aid climbing by providing footholds. Spiked or clawed tops can be effective against uninvited visitors and can also permit a lower fence with equal security. The unbecoming appearance of a number of spiked fence designs may discourage many homeowners from using them, but where maximum security is necessary they are probably justified. (FIGS. 170, 171) A less menacing solution is the 'catcher,' an overhang created by bending out the top of each bar to make the fence difficult to scale.

Color and Finish

Architectural ironwork is a long-term investment that can easily last a hundred years, but proper finish is essential to its life. Cast iron and mild steel, more susceptible to rust than authentic wrought iron, require more care. The question of color and finish for ironwork is surprisingly controversial among professionals. Much early English ironwork is said to have been painted blue or green and set off with gold.[23] It is hard to imagine a gaudier sight! Samuel Yellin felt wrought iron should be waxed or rubbed with linseed oil to preserve its color, texture, and sharp details. He opposed painting iron any color because paint covers the subtleties and marks of hand craftsmanship. This is particularly true of wrought iron, of course, which was Yellin's medium.[24]

Wrought iron can even be polished, like armor, to a finish bright as silver; over time it acquires a fine patina. To obtain a natural finish on hot rolled steel, one must first remove the 'mill scale' by sanding or sand blasting; a bright polished finish will result. To put on a transparent finish, apply a beeswax and turpentine mixture, rubbing the finish when the turpentine has evaporated; this should be repeated every two to four months. An alternative formula is to use $\frac{5}{6}$ turpentine and $\frac{1}{6}$ fat oil varnish.[25] A simpler, perhaps less attractive, solution is to use spar varnish, but this, too, would require more maintenance than would paint. Lovely

Design: Practical Considerations

FIGURE 170

For someone seeking maximum security, iron spikes offer one solution. Here the wrought iron spikes guard the top of a high fence and prevent access to a side porch of a house. This effective defense is perhaps too forbidding for many homeowners. (Charleston, S.C.; 48 Meeting Street)

FIGURE 171

Delicate wrought iron claws are effectively used to prevent access from a neighboring balcony. Apart from their defensive function, these claws suggest movement like that of birds in flight. (New Orleans, 524 Royal Street)

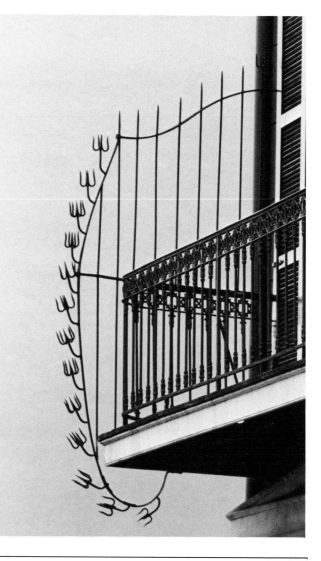

authentic finishes are for the true iron aficionado who can lavish consistent care on an iron collection.

In many cases, paint may be the only solution. If you paint, first cover the ironwork in red oxide, red lead, or other rust-resisting paint; then apply a finish coat of flat alkyd paint—not high gloss enamel or latex—of chemical composition compatible with the rust coat. Although glossy enamel paints may be somewhat more durable, flat paints are preferable for iron because they look more solid and make it easier to read the patterns. With flat paint the iron is a solid, three-dimensional, space-consuming form expressing its great strength. Glossy paint causes reflected light to eat into the visual form; the shiny surface also creates an image inconsistent with the strength of iron.

In no case should paint be applied thickly; this obscures detail and causes unsightly drips, and thick paint also chips easily. Two thin coats are preferable to one thick coat. Minimal paint should be applied in any case so that detail is preserved. Much ironwork has been over-painted, too often in high gloss enamel; after a century of layers it is difficult to even read the pattern. Paint should be stripped from iron that has been buried in it. Use paint remover, wire brush, and rags.

On the question of color there is some consensus. Flat black is always safe and acceptable. In Savannah and Charleston, interesting tones other than black are used—deep rich grays and gray browns. In general, ironwork should not be painted the same color as the architecture it relates to, for this causes the iron to blend in with the architecture and diminishes its ornamental presence and strength.

Poor iron design cannot be corrected by paint, but a sensitive paint job can render ugly ironwork slightly less conspicuous. Offensive ironwork that is painted to match architecture blends in rather than setting itself off as a separate element. This treatment, of course, will compromise any architectural distinction the building may have had. A better alternative is to paint the ironwork a contrasting but related tone darker than the building; the ironwork will remain distinct. Needless to say, the only real solution is to improve the ironwork.

Design: Practical Considerations

Repairs to Old Ironwork

Incorrect repairs often mar fine ironwork permanently. One should always attempt to use the technique and pattern of the original ironworker. Compared with wrought iron or mild steel, cast ironwork is more difficult to repair, being brittle and more difficult to weld. Cast iron repairs are thus better handled in the workshop than in the field.

It is best to minimize the necessity for repairs by preventing rust, but other causes of damage may not be preventable. If a car runs into your hundred-year-old cast iron fence, there is going to be considerable damage! Be sure your insurance policy provides for true replacement or repair rather than merely substitution, which may be inferior. Don't let anyone tell you that your ironwork cannot be replaced; it *can*, but true replacement may be expensive.

Detailing

Contemporary techniques for joining iron are quite different from those of eighteenth- and nineteenth-century iron masters. Arc and torch welds, despised by traditional craftsmen, are the typical methods of joinery today. When they are used, care must be taken to avoid burning into the iron; neither should the weld create surface lumps. Welds should be filed smooth. For wrought ironwork, traditional hammered welds, rivets, clips, screws, bolts, pins, or collars are considered superior by many ironworkers (see Chapter 2); but, despite the superior appearance of these connections, the economy and strength of the modern torch and arc welds cannot be denied.

Two or more parallel iron bars should never be joined directly on top of each other. It is difficult to protect the inner faces from rust. Moreover, in cold climates, water that enters the interstices will expand in freezing and deform the iron. Much ironwork in Boston, of otherwise excellent craftsmanship, has become misshapen for this reason.

Braces and Footings

Design of supporting braces of fences, balconies, fire escapes, or other ironwork should not be neglected. When treated as integral visual members, supporting members can contribute greatly to the esthetic value of the piece. Unseen but crucial elements that could be ignored, to your grandchildren's sorrow, are the footings for heavy ironwork such as fences and gates. Too often we see sagging, tipping fences and gates whose designers failed to consider the weight and stress of their ironwork. Heavy ironwork requires reinforced concrete footings below the frost line.

Economic Considerations

The major cost in architectural ironwork today is labor. At least seven design factors appreciably affect the cost of producing wrought ironwork:

1
Number of connections: the more connections a design contains, the higher the cost.

2
Type of connections: arc and torch welds are usually less expensive than rivet, collar, screw, bolt, pin, or hammer-welded connections. Welds should be ground smooth, and this will add somewhat to the cost.

3
Number of bends: it is more economical to use a few large bends than numerous small bends.

4
Uniformity of bends: the more numerous the bends of different shape, the higher the cost will be.

5
Number of pieces that must be cut: the fewer the cut pieces, the lower the costs; however, cuts are probably less expensive than bends.

6
Amount of forging or hammering involved: elaborate skilled forge work, although beautiful, will be expensive.

7
Weight of stock: very heavy ironwork (over one hundred pounds) requires the labor of two or more men to fabricate and install, a factor in its cost. As an example, consider that a fence panel of ½ inch square iron can be handled by one man; when the iron is increased to ⅝ inch or more, two or more men are usually needed. Stock less than ½ inch square usually takes less time to work, but the cost difference for the iron is small; the greater strength and improved appearance of heavier iron usually offsets the somewhat higher cost of heavier stock.

Design: Practical Considerations

Although many nineteenth-century designs would be very expensive to reproduce today, nearly anyone can afford respectable ironwork. In developing designs for an iron installation one should bear in mind the factors affecting the costs. Wrought iron patterns with only straight pieces and no hammering can be attractive and quite economical. (FIG. 172) Some of these are limited to architecture that can take a severe and modern-looking design. Cast iron, though expensive to produce on a small scale, is, when mass produced, still less expensive than most wrought iron. For a list of several companies making cast iron components, see Chapter 10.

Traditional wrought ironwork, while not unobtainable today, requires skills only a few craftsmen possess or are willing to develop. If possible hire a good architect to design your ironwork. When selecting an ironworker, be sure to examine some of his previous output; don't rely on his word that he can reproduce a nineteenth-century pattern. Judge for yourself his design quality, workmanship, and installation. Examine the visual quality of welded or other connections. Be sure, too, that the ironwork has been attached neatly and securely to the building without damaging the exterior walls or detailing.

To develop your own sensitivity, it is important to study a few examples of high quality ironwork. The best work will usually appear in historic neighborhoods and on older public buildings. If you are unsure where to find examples, contact your local museum, architectural society, or historic preservation group.

FIGURE 172
This is a good example of a simple and economical iron pattern. Its geometric contemporary style could be used with many unadorned twentieth-century buildings as well as in historic architecture. By using straight unbent stock, the ironworker minimizes his difficulties. This pattern can easily be reproduced anywhere in the United States. (Boston, 23–25 Union Park; fabricated by Weld Rite Ornamental Iron, 1973)

Design: Practical Considerations

9 Patternbook

PATTERN I
Fence; adapted from gate design by Luis Barragan, Mexico, D.F.

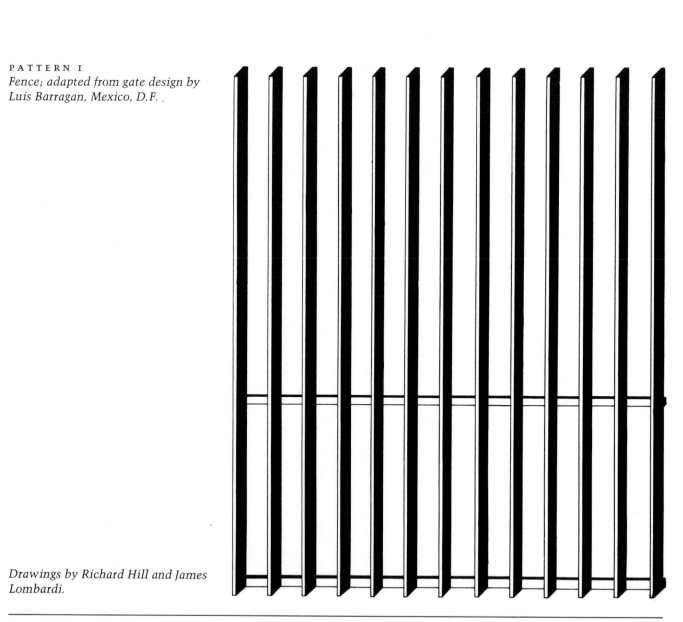

Drawings by Richard Hill and James Lombardi.

PATTERN 2
*Fence; 57 Commonwealth Avenue,
Boston; house built 1874, Carl Feh-
mer, Architect.*

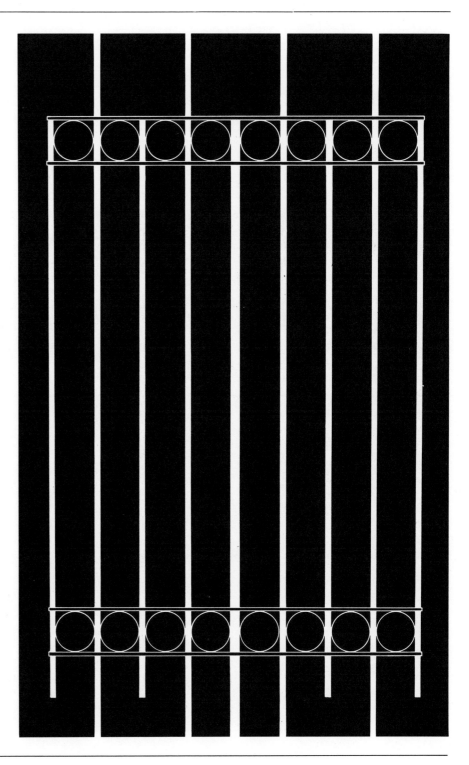

Patternbook

PATTERN 3
Stair rail; 1221 Spruce Street, Philadelphia.

PATTERN 4
Stair rail; 216 South Ninth Street, Philadelphia.

Ornamental Ironwork

PATTERN 5
Bull's eye window guard; City Hall,
80 Broad Street, Charleston, S.C.;
built 1801, attributed to Gabriel Man-
nigault, Architect.

PATTERN 6
Balcony railing; 60 Meeting Street,
Charleston, S.C.

Fence; 6 Joy Street, Boston; house built 1824, Alexander Parris, Architect.

PATTERN 8
Fence; design by the authors.

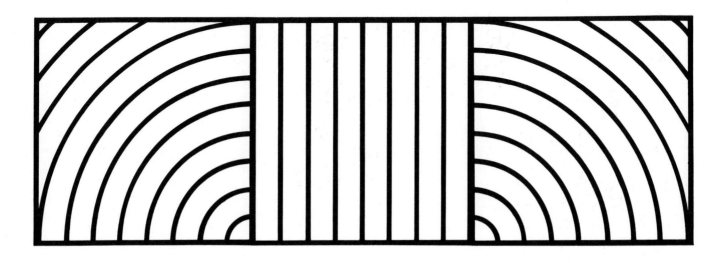

*Balcony railing; adapted from railing
at 411 Royal Street, New Orleans.*

Fence; adapted from fence at 6113
Germantown Avenue, Philadelphia.

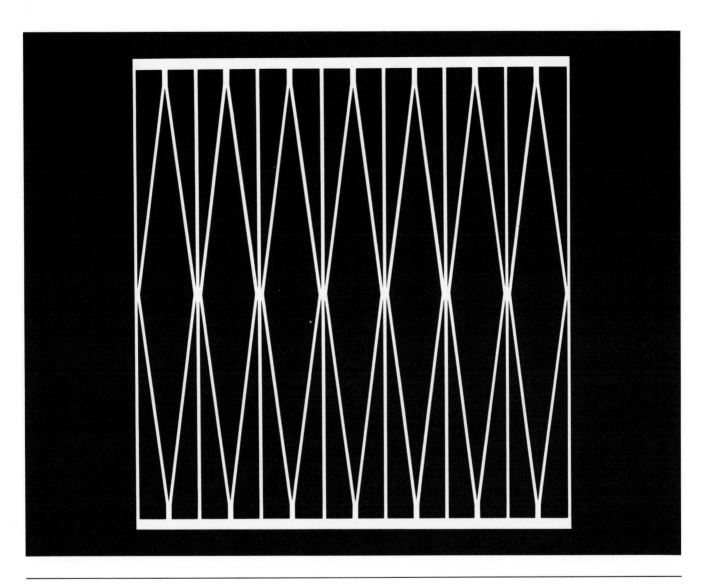

Fence and stair rail; 23–25 Union Park, South End, Boston.

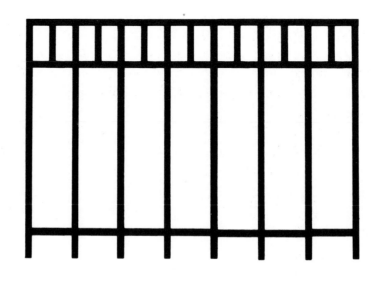

Ornamental Ironwork

PATTERN 12
Double gates; design by the authors.

PATTERN 13
"Bulfinch" pattern; fence panel
adapted from design at 85 Mount Ver-
non Street, 45 Beacon Street, and 75,
77, 79, and 83 Pinckney Street.

PATTERN 14
Fence; adapted from fence at 12 Fair-field Street, Boston; house built 1879, Cabot & Chandler, Architects.

PATTERN 15
Low garden fence; 115 Common-wealth Avenue, Boston; house built 1876, Cummings & Sears, Architects.

Ornamental Ironwork

Fence; 34 Mount Vernon Street, Boston; house built 1822.

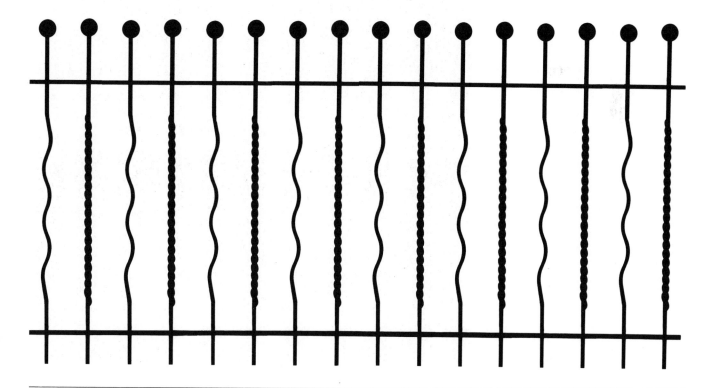

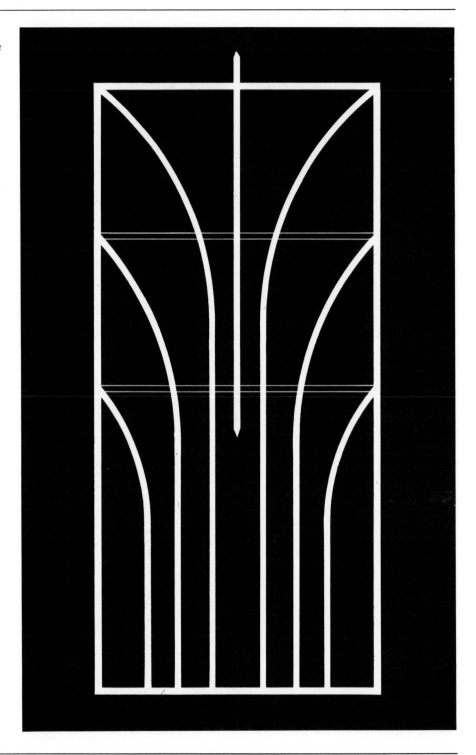

Window and door guard; 43 Commonwealth Avenue, Boston; design by the authors, 1974.

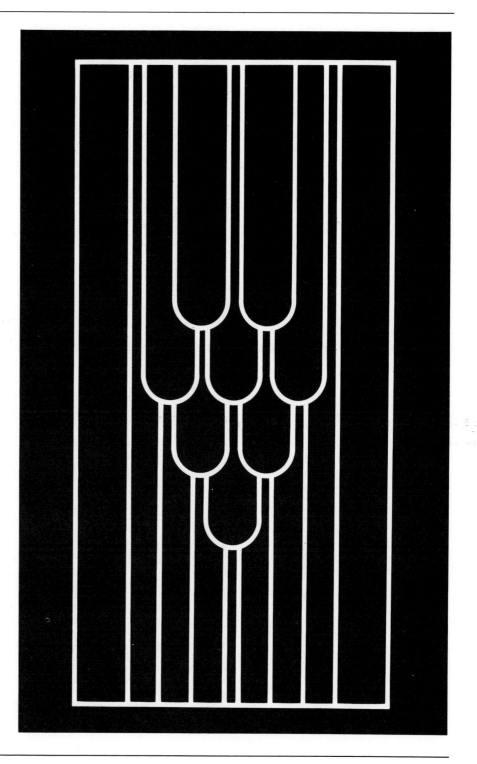

Window or door guard; design by the authors.

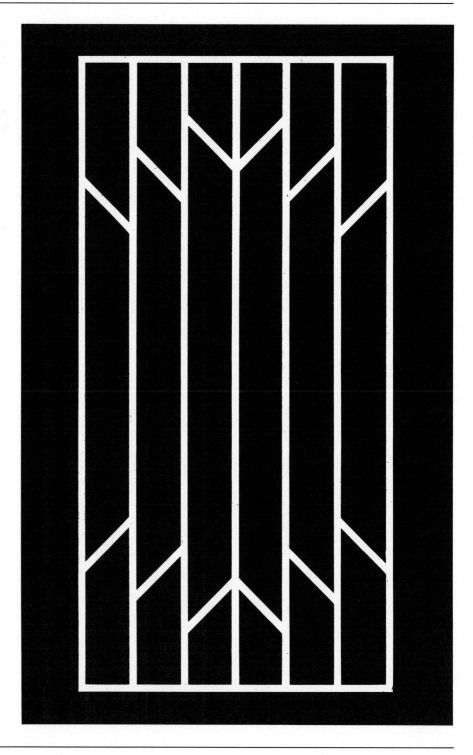

Ornamental Ironwork

Ironwork Resources

ORGANIZATIONS AND FOUNDATIONS

Artist-Blacksmiths' Association of North America (ABANA)
P.O. Box 1181
Nashville, Indiana 47448
Phone: 812-988-6919

ABANA has a large membership of artist-blacksmiths across the country. Names and addresses of members may be obtained from the Association or from its regional chapters. Since mailing addresses of regional chapters change frequently, only the names are listed below.

Alabama Forge Council

Appalachian Area Chapter of ABANA (Tennessee)

Appalachian Blacksmiths' Association (West Virginia)

Arizona Artist-Blacksmiths' Association

Blacksmiths' Association of Missouri

Blacksmiths' Guild of Central Maryland

Blacksmiths' Guild of the Potomac (Virginia)

California Blacksmiths' Association

Florida Artist-Blacksmiths' Association

Great Plains Blacksmiths' Association (Kansas)

Guild of Metalsmiths (Minnesota)

Illinois Valley Blacksmiths' Association

Indiana Blacksmiths' Association

Inland Northwest Blacksmiths' Association (Washington)

Kentucky Blacksmiths' Association

Maritime Artist-Blacksmiths' Association (Nova Scotia)

Michigan Artist-Blacksmiths' Association

Mid-Atlantic Smiths' Association (Pennsylvania)

Mississippi Forge Council

New England Blacksmiths (New Hampshire)

New York State Designer-Blacksmiths

North Carolina Chapter of ABANA

Northeastern Blacksmiths' Association (New York)

Northwest Blacksmiths' Association (Washington)

Northwest Ohio Blacksmiths

Ontario Artist-Blacksmiths' Association

Oregon Chapter of ABANA

Pennsylvania Artist-Blacksmiths' Association

Pittsburgh Area Artist-Blacksmiths

Prairie Blacksmiths' Association (Nebraska)

Rocky Mountain Smiths (Colorado)

Southern Ohio Forge and Anvil

Southwest Artist-Blacksmiths' Association (New Mexico)

Texas Artist-Blacksmiths' Association

Tullie Smiths Blacksmiths' Guild (Georgia)

Upper Midwest Blacksmiths' Association (Wisconsin)

Western Canadian Blacksmiths (Alberta)

American Crafts Council
44 West 53rd Street
New York, New York 10019

American Iron and Steel Institute
1000 16th Street N.W.
Washington, D.C. 20056

Cast Metals Federation
Cast Metals Federation Building
20611 Center Ridge Road
Rocky River, Ohio 44116

The Francis Whitaker Educational
Blacksmiths' Foundation
1493 County Road 106
Carbondale, Colorado 81623
Phone: 303-963-9386

Grants to blacksmiths for education-
related projects, archives, and other
activities to promote the art and craft
of blacksmithing.

Friends of Cast Iron Architecture
235 East 87th Street
New York, New York 10028
Phone: 212-369-6004

Iron Castings Society
Cast Metals Federation Building
20611 Center Ridge Road
Rocky River, Ohio 44116

National Ornamental and
Miscellaneous Metals Association
(NOMMA)
804-810 Main Street, Suite E
Forest Park, Georgia 30050

Office of Technical Preservation
Services
National Park Service
Preservation Assistance Division
P.O. Box 37127
Washington, D.C. 20013-7127
Phone: 202-343-9573

Publications, seminars, and grants for
preservation.

JOURNALS

Anvil
P.O. Box 1810
Georgetown, California 95634
Phone: 916-333-2142

The Anvil's Ring
P.O. Box 212
Morgantown, West Virginia 26505

The Fabricator
National Ornamental and
Miscellaneous Metals Association

804-810 Main Street, Suite E
Forest Park, Georgia 30050

Forge Facts
P.O. Box 1212
Breckenridge, Colorado 80424.
Phone: 303-453-4477

MUSEUMS

National Ornamental Metal Museum
374 West California
Memphis, Tennessee 38106
Phone: 901-774-6380

BOOKS AND SUPPLIES

Centaur Forge, Ltd.
117 North Spring Street
Burlington, Wisconsin 53105
Phone: 414-763-9175

Blacksmiths' equipment, books, and
supplies.

Iron Age Antiques
Route 1, Box 169
Ocean View, Delaware 19970
Phone: 302-539-5344

Hand and power forging tools,
old books on blacksmithing and
ironwork, old tools.

Norm Larson
5426 Highway 246
Lampoc, California 93436
Phone: 805-735-2095

Books on the art of blacksmithing,
new and antiquarian.

SCHOOLS OF BLACKSMITHING

Anderson Ranch
Brad Miller, Director
Box 5598
Snowmass Village, Colorado 81615
Phone: 303-923-3181

Art League School
Gerri Gordon, Director
105 N. Union Street
Arlington, Virginia 22314
Phone: 703-683-2323

Brookfield Craft Center
Jack Russel, Director
P.O. Box 122, Route 25
Brookfield, Connecticut 06804

Cedar Lakes Craft Center
Tim Pyles, Director
Ripley, West Virginia 25271
Phone: 304-372-7005

Center for Craftsmanship
Jim Bjornerud, Director
245 Tech Wing, Jarvis Hall
University of Wisconsin-Stout
Menomonie, Wisconsin 54751
Phone: 715-232-1102

Cranbrook Academy of Art
Roy Flade, President
500 Lone Pine Road, Box 801
Bloomfield Hills, Michigan 48013
Phone: 313-645-3300

The Francis Whitaker Blacksmithing
School
1493 County Road 106
Carbondale, Colorado 81623
Phone: 303-963-9386

Glen Echo Park Classes
% National Park Service
7300 MacArthur Boulevard
Glen Echo, Maryland 20812
Phone: 301-492-6282

Haystack Mountain School of Crafts
Francis Merritt, Director
Deer Isle, Maine 04627-0087
Phone: 207-348-2306

Montgomery College
Rockville Campus
51 Mannakee Street
Rockville, Maryland 20850
Phone: 301-279-5040

Pioneer Crafts Council
Eleanor Molnar, Director
P.O. Box 2141
Uniontown, Pennsylvania 15401
Phone: 412-438-2811

Rhode Island School of Design
14 College Street
Providence, Rhode Island 02903
Phone: 401-331-3511

Southwest Craft Center
Ric Collier, Director
300 Augusta Street
San Antonio, Texas 78205
Phone: 512-224-1848

Turley Forge
Route 10, Box 88C
Santa Fe, New Mexico 87501
Phone: 505-471-8608

The University of the Arts
Peter Solmssen, President
Broad and Pine Streets
Philadelphia, Pennsylvania 19102
Phone: 215-875-4808

University of Washington
School of Art
320 Schmitz Hall
1400 Northeast Campus Parkway
Seattle, Washington 98195
Phone: 206-543-0970

Washington University
School of Fine Arts
1 Brookings Drive
St. Louis, Missouri 63130
Phone: 314-991-2149

DIRECTORY OF IRONWORKERS

This directory has been compiled from a variety of sources including personal references, publications, and responses to a questionnaire sent to ornamental ironworkers in major cities in the United States and *Canada. It is impossible to judge the quality of work in a survey, however the directory does provide a starting point in the search for an ornamental iron manufacturer. Names are organized alphabetically, first by state, then by town or city.*

United States

Alabama

Lawler Machine & Foundry Company
4908 Powell Avenue
Birmingham, Alabama 35222
Phone: 205-595-0596

Ornamental designs in cast iron and aluminum.

Holman Iron Works
Highway 231 North
Montgomery, Alabama 36110
Phone: 205-272-2950

Many types of ornamental ironwork.

Arizona

Adobe Wrought Iron
4118 East University Drive
Phoenix, Arizona 85034
Phone: 602-437-2999

All types of ironwork including spiral stairways.

Arkansas

Cagle Ornamental Iron Works
1708 Towson
Fort Smith, Arkansas 72901
Phone: 501-785-5172

Ornamental ironwork; custom fire screens a specialty.

California

David Nourot
155 East I Street
Benicia, California 94510
Phone: 707-745-1133

Forged and welded ornamental ironwork.

Jerry Coe
1214 Fourth Street
Berkeley, California 94710
Phone: 415-527-2950

Daniel Dole, Artist-Blacksmith
1101 10th Street
Berkeley, California 94710
Phone: 415-524-4728

Guadalajara Imports, Inc.
117 North Brea Boulevard
Brea, California 92621
Phone: 714-529-9075 or 213-691-7294

Forged and bent ironwork.

Chris Axelson
P.O. Box 222598
Carmel, California 93922
Phone: 408-624-3909

John Hudson
Route 1, Box 66
Carmel, California 93923
Phone: 408-624-1010

Fritz Hagist
34895 Kruse Ranch Road
Cazadero, California 95421
Phone: 707-847-3362

Lowell Chaput
8428 Lakewood Drive
Cotati, California 94928
Phone: 707-795-0429

Decoart
600 North Robertson Boulevard
Los Angeles, California 90069
Phone: 213-657-0891

Importer of old and antique European wrought ironwork.

Mildred
4036 Moore Street
Los Angeles, California 90066
Phone: 213-305-1218

Murray's Iron Works
Showroom: 8632 Melrose Avenue
Los Angeles, California 90069
Phone: 213-652-0632
Workshop: 5915 Blackwelder Street
Culver City, California 90232
Phone: 213-839-7737

One of the largest companies in the country specializing in European style blacksmithing.

Michael Bondi
1818 Shorey Street
Oakland, California 94607
Phone: 415-763-1327

Forged metal work in iron, copper, brass, and bronze.

Eric Clausen
5401 Claremont Avenue
Oakland, California 94618
Phone: 415-655-8428

Sculptural ironwork, whimsical forging; fences, gates, window guards, chandeliers, furniture, repoussé work.

Ken Gilliland
1440 29th Avenue
Oakland, California 94601
Phone: 415-533-6739

Phoenix Iron Works
888 Cedar Street
Oakland, California 94607
Phone: 415-465-9900

Lampposts, park benches, newel posts, hitching posts and architectural items in cast iron, brass, bronze, and aluminum.

William Roan
1805 East 14th Street
Oakland, California 94606

Dave Reis
393 A Elysian Avenue
Penngrove, California 94951
Phone: 707-664-8504

Toby Hickman
6030 Roblar Road
Petaluma, California 94952
Phone: 707-664-8910

Robert Owings
121 H Street
Petaluma, California 94952
Phone: 707-778-8261

Monte Haberman
1202 East Pine Street
Placentia, California 92670
Phone: 714-993-4766

Forged ornamental ironwork.

Hech A Mano Ornamental Iron
1401 Cutting Boulevard
Richmond, California 94804
Phone: 415-236-9458

Lucia Eames Demetrios
2 20th Avenue
San Francisco, California 94121
Phone: 415-788-3461

Custom designed fences, gates, grates in flat cut bronze or steel.

Renaissance Forge
47 Juniper Street
San Francisco, California 94103
Phone: 415-864-6033

Ornamental forged ironwork.

The Village Ironworks
1201 West San Carlos Street
San Jose, California 95126
Phone: 408-293-7080

Ridge Foundry
1554 Doolittle Drive
San Leandro, California 94577
Phone: 415-352-0551

Cast iron.

Stephen Bondi
433 Grant Street
Santa Cruz, California 95060
Phone: 408-423-8433

E. A. Chase
P.O. Box 785
Santa Cruz, California 95060
Phone: 408-423-3188

Michael Chisham
1232 Cleveland
Santa Rosa, California 95401
Phone: 707-578-7198

James Hubbell Art Studio
930 Orchard Lane
Santa Ysabel, California 92070
Phone: 619-765-0171

Original forged ironwork designs; bronze, stained glass.

Carl Jennings
3500 Westach Way
Sonoma, California 95476
Phone: 707-938-5493

Art Jones
1936 Georgia Street
Vallejo, California 94590
Phone: 707-552-2548

Richard Schrader
1576 Montgomery
Vista, California 92083
Phone: 619-941-1978

Doug Carmichael
6850 Third Gate Road
Willits, California 95490

Custom ornamental metalwork.

Jere Kirkpatrick
300 East San Francisco Street
Willits, California 95490
Phone: 707-459-2523

Colorado

Craig May
68 Rim Rock Road
Bailey, Colorado 80421
Phone: 303-674-5702

Myers and Company
P.O. 1025
Basalt, Colorado 81621
Phone: 303-927-4761

Custom ornamental blacksmithing including furniture, lighting fixtures, fences, gates, window grilles, and other architectural pieces.

Jim Fleming, The Mountain Anvil
Box 1212
Breckenridge, Colorado 80424
Phone: 303-453-4477

Ornamental architectural bronze, iron, and steel.

Bill Dawe
1367 Barber Drive
Carbondale, Colorado 81623
Phone: 303-963-1675

Jim Hoffman
Box 816
Carbondale, Colorado 81623
Phone: 303-963-1930

Francis Whitaker
1493 County Road 106
Carbondale, Colorado 81623
Phone: 303-963-9386

Custom designed hand forged ironwork using historic European techniques; no art welding.

Bruce MacMillan
12604 U.S. Highway 285
Conifer, Colorado 80433
Phone: 303-838-7951

Architectural blacksmithing in bronze and iron.

Weatherguard Ornamental Iron
6890 South Emporia
Englewood, Colorado 80112
Phone: 303-790-8808

Door and window guards, railings, decorative forged and cast columns, ornamental iron patio cover structures.

Connecticut

Post Road Iron Works, Inc.
345 West Putman Avenue
Greenwich, Connecticut 06830
Phone: 203-869-6322

Forged and bent ironwork; historic reproductions.

Kenneth Lynch & Sons
Box 488
Wilton, Connecticut 06897

Weathervanes, park benches, garden ornaments, sundials, lighting fixtures.

Florida

Continental Iron, Inc.
1635 West 31st Place
Hialeah, Florida 33012
Phone: 305-823-9051

Security ironwork.

David Ponsler
Wonderland Products, Inc.
P.O. Box 6074
Jacksonville, Florida 32236

Artist-blacksmith creating ornamental architectural ironwork, lanterns, furniture, and other objects.

Van Sickle's Ornamental Iron
5044 Edwards Street
Jacksonville, Florida 32205
Phone: 904-786-0555

Ornamental and security ironwork.

Griffiths Metal Products, Inc.
10461 Southwest 184th Terrace
Miami, Florida 33157
Phone: 305-233-6916

Ornamental iron and aluminum; spiral stairways a specialty.

M & H Ornamental Iron Work
1135 Northwest 54th Street
Miami, Florida 33127
Phone: 305-751-7862

Floridian Forge
3129 Northeast 14th Street
Ocala, Florida 32670
Phone: 904-629-2776

Custom work only using original or architect's designs; reproductions; circular stairways a specialty.

Klahm & Sons, Inc.
2151 Northeast Jacksonville Road
Ocala, Florida 32670
Phone: 904-622-6565

Ray Nager
5712 West Sligh Avenue
Tampa, Florida 33634
Phone: 813-886-8765

Forged architectural ironwork and sculpture.

Georgia

Ivan Bailey
887 West Marietta Street N.W.
Atlanta, Georgia 30318
Phone: 404-874-7674

Walker Street Ornamental Iron
201 Simpson Street N.W.
Atlanta, Georgia 30313
Phone: 404-688-2098

Forged iron reproductions.

Gary Noffke
P.O. Box 776
Farmington, Georgia 30638
Phone: 404-542-1657

Forged stainless steel; custom design pieces.

Idaho

Nahum Hersom
3011 Innis Street
Boise, Idaho 83703
Phone: 208-345-9163

Ornamental forged ironwork including French repoussé work.

Illinois

Ace Iron Works, Inc.
510 West Pershing Road
Chicago, Illinois 60609
Phone: 312-373-1344

Ornamental ironwork; window guards.

H & Bros. Custom Ornamental Iron Works
4835 Southwestern Boulevard
Chicago, Illinois 60609
Phone: 312-778-7118

Mueller Ornamental Iron Works, Inc.
3632 North Cicero Avenue
Chicago, Illinois 60641
Phone: 312-286-2278

Kansas

Bob's Ornamental Iron
734 Southwest Boulevard
Kansas City, Kansas 66103
Phone: 913-236-4444

Custom forged ironwork.

Quality Ornamental Iron, Inc.
7126 Kaw Drive
Kansas City, Kansas 66111
Phone: 913-299-0167

Kentucky

Kentucky Ornamental Iron
1047 Goodwin Drive
Lexington, Kentucky 40505
Phone: 606-255-7791

Iron, brass, and aluminum fabricators.

Iowa

Grosse Steel Company
2225 Lincoln Street
Cedar Falls, Iowa 50613
Phone: 319-277-5900

All types of ornamental iron.

Louisiana

Abel Ornamental Iron Works
2315 Tyler Street
Kenner, Louisiana 70062
Phone: 504-467-3494

Cast iron gates, window guards, columns, balconies, and stairs.

Authement's Ornamental Iron Works
1415 27th Street
Kenner, Louisiana 70062
Phone: 504-467-6666

Maine

The Ram's Head Forge
34A Fish Street
Fryeburg, Maine 04037
Phone: 207-697-2011

Hand forged early American and contemporary ironwork.

Massachusetts

Boston Design Corporation
100 Magazine Street
Boston, Massachusetts 02119
Phone: 617-442-6118

Spiral stairways and steel fireplaces are specialties.

Weld-Rite Ornamental Iron
3371 Washington Street, Rear
Jamaica Plain, Massachusetts 02130
Phone: 617-524-9747

Forged iron; spiral stairways a specialty.

Old Mansions Company
1305 Blue Hill Avenue
Mattapan, Massachusetts 02126
Phone: 617-296-0737

Large collections of antique and period gates, fencing, balconies, lighting.

Santini Brothers Iron Works, Inc.
9 Cooper Street
Medford, Massachusetts 02155
Phone: 617-396-1450

Fences, stair rails, and window guards are specialties.

Norris H. Tripp and Company, Inc.
253 Cedar Street
New Bedford, Massachusetts 02740
Phone: 508-993-3222

Ornamental sheet metal finials, flashings, and detailing.

DeAngelis Ironwork, Inc.
305 Depot Street
South Easton, Massachusetts 02375
Phone: 508-238-4310

Cast and forged historic reproductions; work includes the reproduction cast iron fence around the Boston Public Garden.

Newton Millham
672 Drift Road
Westport, Massachusetts 02790
Phone: 617-636-5437

Hand forged architectural hardware for historic buildings.

Edlin and Son
33 Rockdale Street
Worcester, Massachusetts 01606
Phone: 508-852-3383

Forged iron historic reproductions; work is totally forged—no modern welding, no phony colonial; door and fireplace equipment a specialty.

Michigan

Ideal Wrought Iron
7839 Greenfield Road
Detroit, Michigan 48228
Phone: 313-581-1324

Cast and forged rails, columns, and window guards.

Minnesota

Loftus Ornamental Iron
2340 Louisiana Avenue North
Minneapolis, Minnesota 55427
Phone: 612-545-2669

Superior Iron, Inc.
12015 Brockton Lane
Osseo, Minnesota 55369
Phone: 612-428-2211

Missouri

Forge Master Iron Company
7255 Metropolitan Boulevard
Barnhart, Missouri 63012
Phone: 314-464-2800

Forged ironwork; fences, railings, reproductions, light fixtures, custom designs.

Conner and Associates, Inc.
4801 Oleatha
St. Louis, Missouri 63116
Phone: 314-481-8030

Florissant Ornamental Iron Works
325 St. Francis Street
St. Louis, Missouri 63031
Phone: 314-837-3363

Custom iron work; log racks, railings, stairways.

New Hampshire

Dimitri Gerakaris
The Upper Gates Road
North Canaan, New Hampshire 03741
Phone: 603-523-7366

Custom designed, site specific forged architectural and sculptural metalsmithing from enormous to small in size.

New Jersey

Julius Blum & Company, Inc.
P.O. Box 292
Carlstadt, New Jersey 07072
Phone: 201-438-4600

Stock elements for ornamental metal work.

Les Mettalliers Champenois—USA
L.M.C. Corporation
118 2nd Avenue
Paterson, New Jersey 07514
Phone: 201-279-3573

Artistic iron and metal work; restoration and original designs.

New Mexico

Tom Joyce Architectural Blacksmithing
Route 9, Box 73J
Santa Fe, New Mexico 87505
Phone: 505-982-0485

Forged architectural ironwork.

Turley Forge
Route 10, Box 88C
Santa Fe, New Mexico 87501
Phone: 505-471-8608

Blacksmithing school; hand forged, custom designed builders' hardware, grilles, railings, gates, reproduction ironwork; southwestern Spanish-Colonial ironware; branding irons.

New York

Schwartz's Forge and Metalworks
P.O. Box 205, Forge Hollow Road
Deansboro, New York 13328
Phone: 315-841-4477

Aesthetica/Roland C. Greefkes
P.O. Box 14
Gilbertsville, New York 13776
Phone: 607-783-2114

Third-generation artist-blacksmith; original designs.

Markusen Metalsmithing Studio
17218 Roosevelt Highway
Kendall, New York 14476
Phone: 716-659-8001

Forged and fabricated ornamental ironwork for interior and exterior architectural applications.

Albert Paley
25 North Washington Street
Rochester, New York 14614
Phone: 716-232-5260

Artist working in steel and other metals; all works are unique creative pieces of art; work has included gates, fences, window guards, furniture, jewelry, and sculpture.

Infinity Forge
Marte Cellura
6123 Ridge Road
Sodus, New York 14551
Phone: 315-483-6189

Hand forged art and craft items; architectural commissions; custom made fireplace tools of wood and brass.

North Carolina

Kayne & Son
76 Daniel Ridge Road
Box 275A
Candler, North Carolina 28715
Phone: 704-667-8868

Hand forged iron hardware.

Ohio

Historical Fence and Ironworks
P.O. Box 141459
Cincinnati, Ohio 45250
Phone: 513-244-1442

Reproductions of nineteenth-century ironwork; send $2 for catalogue.

Oregon

Mascotte Home Security Products
9106 Southeast 82nd Street
Portland, Oregon 97266
Phone: 503-771-1282

Hand rails, garden gates, security guards.

Pennsylvania

M. Cohen and Sons, Inc.
Box 547, 400 Reed Road
Broomall, Pennsylvania 19008
Phone: 215-544-7100

Forged iron, spiral staircases; spiral stair kits.

Robert A. Griffith, Metalsmith
41 Grow Street
Montrose, Pennsylvania 18801
Phone: 717-278-4326

Sculptural ironwork.

Custom Wrought Iron Works
R. D. 2
Oil City, Pennsylvania 16301
Phone: 814-676-4575

Railings, grilles, gates.

Country Iron Foundry
Box 600
Paoli, Pennsylvania 19301
Phone: 215-296-7122

Ornamental cast iron firebacks.

Artline Ornamental
4820 Yocum Street
Philadelphia, Pennsylvania 19143
Phone: 215-727-2923

Forged and bent iron.

Filippi Brothers, Inc.
7720-22 Winston Road
Philadelphia, Pennsylvania 19118
Phone: 215-247-5973

Restoration of Colonial ironwork.

Mayfair Ornamental Iron Co.
4562 Hawthorne Street
Philadelphia, Pennsylvania 19124
Phone: 215-743-1251

Christopher T. Ray Studios
Box 44128
Philadelphia, Pennsylvania 19144
Phone: 215-438-7129

Forged and fabricated custom design architectural ironwork.

Samuel Yellin Metalworkers
5520 Arch Street
Philadelphia, Pennsylvania 19139
Phone: 215-472-3122

Founded by the great Samuel Yellin; custom work in mild steel, brass, bronze, monel, stainless steel, aluminum, and copper.

Groll Ornamental Iron and
Wire Works
1201 Becks Run Road
Pittsburgh, Pennsylvania 15210
Phone: 412-431-4444

Custom residential and church work.

South Carolina

Heritage House
30 Cumberland Street
Charleston, South Carolina 29401
Phone: 803-577-6808

Iron bootscrapers, lamp posts, copper and brass lanterns, gates, fences, Victorian style cast iron garden benches.

Dixie Lighting, Inc.
P.O. Box 5121
Columbia, South Carolina 29250
Phone: 803-771-6344

Iron bootscrapers, lamp posts, copper and brass lanterns, garden lighting, gates, fences, Victorian style cast iron garden benches.

Tennessee

Ethan Industries
5304 Republic Drive
Memphis, Tennessee 38118
Phone: 901-794-3667

Ornamental steel, cast iron, and cast aluminum.

Anderson Metals
1157 Whitten Road
Memphis, Tennessee 38134
Phone: 901-726-6874

Hand forged doors, gates, fire screens, consoles.

Pickle Ornamental Iron Co., Inc.
3177 Summer Avenue
Memphis, Tennessee 38112
Phone: 901-452-3754

Fire screens, columns, railings, custom doors, fences, gates, window guards.

Herndon & Merry, Inc.
519 West Thompson Lane
Nashville, Tennessee 37211
Phone: 615-254-6471

Ornamental stairways, gates, railings, doors, carports, mailboxes.

Barcroft Welding
P.O. Box 16Z
Ripley, Tennessee 38063
Phone: 901-635-3472

Texas

Iron Craft Studio, Inc.
2663 Lombardy Lane
Dallas, Texas 75220
Phone: 214-352-3042

Hand forged ornamental iron; gates, fences, interior balustrades.

Nesbit Metal Company
6721 Maple Avenue
Dallas, Texas 75235
Phone: 214-352-4575

Cast and forged ornamental metalwork.

Jesco Ornamental Iron Works
139 Braniff Street
San Antonio, Texas 78216
Phone: 512-341-7472

Washington

Buser Ornamental Iron Works
1110 North 143rd Street
Seattle, Washington 98133
Phone: 206-367-3376

Mexican Artistic Iron and
Brass Works
2209 West Elmore Street
Seattle, Washington 98199
Phone: 206-285-3607

Forged iron and brass of own design or customer's; one-of-a-kind pieces; gates, fireplace tools and screens, railings, grilles, wall ornaments.

Washington, D.C.

Iron Shop
P.O. Box 48010, N.E.
Washington, D.C. 20002
Phone: 202-546-1985

Columbian Iron Works, Inc.
1401 22nd Street Southeast
Washington, D.C. 20020
Phone: 202-584-6922

Custom design and fabrication of forged iron gates, guards, interior and exterior ornamental work.

Wisconsin

Postville Blacksmith Shop
Route 1, Box 51A
Blanchardville, Wisconsin
Phone: 608-527-2494

Tom Wilson
North 69 West 5425 Bridge Road
Cedarburg, Wisconsin 53012

Forged architectural metalwork, antique ironwork repair and restoration, forged tools.

Eric Moebius
421 South Second Street
Milwaukee, Wisconsin 53204
Phone: 414-347-0545

Custom forged metalwork in iron, bronze, copper, stainless steel.

Wyoming

Brent Nichols
1400 East College
Cheyenne, Wyoming 82007

Fabricated architectural ironwork.

Canada

Central Iron Works, Inc.
4115 Mentana
Montreal, Quebec H2L 3S5
Phone: 514-524-5733

Art Smithing Iron Works
100 Brydon Drive
Rexdale, Ontario M9W 4N9
Phone: 416-742-3312

Custom handcrafted blacksmithing; lighting fixtures, furniture, gates, railings.

Spanish Iron Works
6850 Boulevard Couture
St. Leonard 458, Quebec H1P 2W6
Phone: 514-326-0721

Notes

1
Much of the material in this section is based on the following works, cited in our References: Bollinger, *Elementary Wrought Iron; Wrought Ironwork: A Manual of Instruction for Craftsmen,* by the Council for Small Industries in Rural Areas; Geerlings, *Wrought Iron in Architecture;* Lister, *Decorative Wrought Ironwork in Great Britain;* and Underwood, *Creative Wrought Ironwork.*

2
Much of the material in this section is based on Lister's *Decorative Cast Ironwork in Great Britain* (See our References).

3
E. N. Hartley, *Ironworks on the Saugus* (Norman, Okla.: University of Oklahoma Press, 1957).

4
Alston Deas, *The Early Ironwork of Charleston* (Columbia, S.C.: Bostick and Thornley, 1941), p. 27.

5
Lillian Chaplin Bragg, *Old Savannah Ironwork* (Savannah, 1957).

6
Deas, p. 15.

7
In *Early American Wrought Iron* (New York: Charles Scribner's Sons, 1928), Vol. III, Albert H. Sonn disagrees with Alston Deas, calling Iusti Italian, not German.

8
Oscar Handlin, *Boston's Immigrants,* p. 78.

9
John Gloag and Derek Bridgewater, *A History of Cast Iron in Architecture* (London: Allen and Unwin, 1948).

10
Bainbridge Bunting, *Houses of Boston's Back Bay* (Cambridge: Harvard University Press, 1967), pp. 292–294.

11
Gerald K. Geerlings, *Wrought Iron in Architecture* (New York: Scribner's, 1929).

12
Stuart M. Lynn, *New Orleans* (New York: Bonanza, 1949).

13
Ann M. Masson and Lydia J. Owen, *Cast Iron and the Crescent City* (New Orleans: Gallier House, 1975), p. 4.

14
Bragg.

15
Deas, p. 13.

16
Frederick W. Robins, *The Smith: The Traditions and Lore of an Ancient Craft* (London and New York: Rider, 1953).

17
The Samuel Yellin Museum of Ironwork is open by appointment only. Contact Clare Yellin, 5520–24 Arch Street, Philadelphia, Pa. 19139.

18
Encyclopaedia Britannica, p. 679.

19
Ibid., p. 679.

20
Myra T. Davis, *Sketches in Iron: Samuel Yellin . . .* (Washington, D.C.: Dimock Gallery, 1971).

21
Quotations are from *Craft Horizons,* December 1970, pp. 23–25.

22
Behind the Fence, a 16 mm. color/ sound film, 1975, by David Darby, documents the fabrication of Paley's fence for the Hunter Museum of Art, Chattanooga, Tennessee. The film may be obtained from:
Mr. David Darby
75 East Monticello Drive
Kaysville, Utah 84037

23
John Starkie Gardner, *English Ironwork of the XVIIth & XVIIIth Centuries* (London: 1911).

24
Davis.

25
Raymond Lister, *Decorative Wrought Ironwork in Great Britain* (London: Bell and Sons, 1957).

Annotated List of References

Architectural Iron Works of the City of New York
Illustrations of Iron Architecture.
New York, 1865.

Catalog of iron buildings, verandas, balconies, fences, cresting, stairs, lintels, and gates.

Ayrton, Maxwell, and Silcock, Arnold
Wrought Iron and Its Decorative Use.
London: Country Life Ltd., 1929.

Contains a history of wrought iron and good examples of English work.

Benjamin, Asher
Practice of Architecture Containing the Five Orders of Architecture and an Additional Column and Entablature with All Their Elements and Details Explained and Illustrated for the Use of Carpenters and Practical Men.
Boston, 1833; first edition.

An early builders' design guide containing patterns for ironwork seen in Boston and elsewhere.

Bollinger, Joseph Walter
Elementary Wrought Iron.
New York: Bruce Publishing Co., 1930.

A very clear presentation of technique with line illustrations.

Bossaglia, Rossana, and Hammacher, Arno
Mazzucotelli: L'Artista Italiano del Ferro Battuto Liberty.
Milano: Edizioni Il Polifilio, 1971.

A large-format photographic essay on the work of this important art nouveau Italian ironworker.

Bragg, Lillian Chaplin
Old Savannah Ironwork.
Savannah, 1957.

A small book containing some amusing anecdotes about Savannah ironwork; not for the scholar or craftsman.

Braun-Feldweg, Wilhelm
Schmiedeeisen.
Ravensburg, Germany: Otto Maier, 1952.

Many photographs of interesting contemporary German wrought iron.

Bunting, Bainbridge
Houses of Boston's Back Bay.
Cambridge, Mass.: Belknap Press of Harvard University Press, 1967.

Chase Brothers and Company
Chase Brothers Illustrated Catalog of Plain and Ornamental Iron Furniture, Iron Railings, and Bronzed Iron Goods.
Boston, ca. 1859.
Catalogue Number 15.

Depicts a delightful assortment of products: bedsteads, cradles, spittoons, window guards, garden furniture, vases, fountains, lamp posts. Catalogue states that they did mail-order business "to any part of the Union."

Chase Brothers and Company
Illustrated Catalog of Useful and Ornamental Bronzed Iron Goods.
Boston, 1854.

Clouzot, Henri
La Ferronnerie Moderne
Paris: Editions d'Art Ch. Moreau, 1928.
Two volumes.

Large-format books with many photos of interesting Art Deco ironwork.

Cottingham, L. N.
A Collection of Architectural Ornaments and Decorations Selected from the Best Authorities for Use of Architects, Sculptors, Ornamental Painters, Masons, Carvers, Modellers in Plaster, Casters in Metal, Paper Stainers, and Every Business Connected with the Arts of Design.
London, 1821.

Shows Greek ornaments but does not illustrate cast ironwork; simply gives motifs to use in the building arts.

Cottingham, L. N.
The Smith and Founders Director, Containing a Series of Designs and Patterns for Ornamental Iron and Brass Work by Cottingham, Architect.
London, 1824.

Contains many designs for ironwork which inspired work in the United States.

Council for Small Industries in Rural Areas
The Blacksmith's Craft.
London: Council for Small Industries in Rural Areas, 1968.

Council for Small Industries in Rural Areas
Wrought Ironwork: A Manual of Instruction for Craftsmen.
London: Council for Small Industries in Rural Areas, 1968.

One of the best technical manuals available, with step-by-step photos.

Council for Small Industries in Rural Areas
Wrought Ironwork Design Catalog.
London: Council for Small Industries in Rural Areas, 1968.

Patterns for fences and other items; some designs are acceptable, but many are too elaborate or unattractive.

Darby, David W.
Behind the Fence.
1975

Thirty-minute 16 mm. color/sound film showing fabrication of Albert Paley's forged mild steel fence for the Hunter Museum of Art. See note 22 for details.

Davis, Myra Tolmach
Sketches in Iron: Samuel Yellin, American Master of Wrought Iron 1885–1940.
Washington, D.C.: Dimock Gallery of George Washington University, 1971.

A booklet on the work of this master ironworker.

Deas, Alston
The Early Ironwork of Charleston.
Columbia, S.C.: Bostick & Thornley, 1941.

A good discussion of Charleston ironwork, accompanied by pencil drawings.

Gay, John
Introduction by Gavin Stamp.
Cast Iron: Architecture and Ornament, Function and Fantasy.
London: John Murray, 1985.

Photographs of British ornamental cast ironwork.

Gayle, Margot
Cast Iron Architecture in New York; A Photographic Survey.
New York: Dover Publications, 1974.

Primarily concerned with cast iron buildings, but has a few examples of New York architectural ironwork.

Gayle, Margot, David W. Look, and John Waite
Metals in America's Historic Buildings: Uses and Preservation Treatments.
Washington, D.C.: U.S. Department of Interior, Heritage Conservation and Recreation Service, Technical Preservation Services Division, 1980.

A survey of the many applications, problems, and methods related to preservation of architectural metals.

Geerlings, Gerald Kenneth
Wrought Iron in Architecture.
New York: Charles Scribner's Sons, 1929.

Examples of ironwork with discussion of methods.

Gloag, John and Bridgwater, Derek
A History of Cast Iron in Architecture.
London: G. Allen and Unwin, 1948.

Hartley, E. N.
Ironworks on the Saugus.
Norman: University of Oklahoma Press, 1957.

A history of early New England ironworks.

Historic Savannah Foundation, Inc.
Historic Savannah.
Savannah, 1968.

Primarily on Savannah architecture and city design, but contains some information and several photos of ironwork.

Hoever, Otto
A Handbook of Wrought Iron from the Middle Ages to the End of the Eighteenth Century.
New York: Universe Books, 1962.

Contains good photos of European work.

Janes, Kirtland and Company
Illustrated Catalogue of Ornamental Ironwork: Fountains, Statuary, Vases, Urns, Lawn Furniture, Pedestals, Baptismal Fonts, Animals, Veranda, Summer House. 1870.
Reprinted, Princeton: Pyne Press, 1971.

Has no fences or window and door grilles.

Kauffman, Henry J.
Early American Ironware, Cast and Wrought.
Rutland, Vermont: C. E. Tuttle Co., 1966.

Krasser, F. and Company, Architectural Ironworkers
Wrought Ironwork: Grilles, Gates, Andirons, and All Kinds of Ornamental Ironwork.
Boston, early twentieth century (no date given).

Contains illustrations of this company's work.

Kuhn, Fritz
Wrought Iron.
New York: Architectural Book Publishing Company, 1969. London: Harrap, 1982.

Photographs of work by this master craftsman.

Lindsay, John Seymour
An Anatomy of English Wrought Iron.
London: Alec Tiranti, 1964.

Excellent pencil drawings of details and techniques of old English ironwork.

Lister, Raymond
Decorative Cast Ironwork in Great Britain.
London: G. Bell and Sons, Ltd., 1960.

Good information on cast iron process.

Lister, Raymond
Decorative Wrought Ironwork in Great Britain.
London: G. Bell and Sons, Ltd., 1957.

Excellent on English ironwork history and traditional blacksmithing technique.

Lister, Raymond
Hammer and Hand: An Essay on the Ironwork of Cambridge.
Cambridge, England: R. Lister, 1969.

Good discussion of processes; has ink drawings.

Lynn, Stuart M.
New Orleans.
New York: Bonanza Books, 1949.

Contains one section on ironwork, primarily photographs.

MacKay, Robert
'Cast Iron Architecture on Beacon Hill in Boston,' *Antiques Magazine.*
June 1975, pp. 1116–1121.

Magnani, Franco
Ornamental Metalwork.
New York: Universe Books, 1967.

Contains some interesting modern Italian iron designs.

Masson, Ann M., and Owen, Lydia J.
Cast Iron and the Crescent City.
New Orleans: Gallier House, 1975.

McIntyre, A. McVoy
Beacon Hill: A Walking Tour.
Boston: Little, Brown, 1975.

Meilach, Dona Z.
Decorative and Sculptural Ironwork.
New York: Crown Publishers, 1977.

Largely non-architectural ironwork.

Pedrini, Augusto
Il Ferro Battuto Sbalzato e Cesellato nell'Arte Italiana dal Secolo Undicesimo al Secolo Diciottesimo.
Milan: Ulrico Hoepli, Editore, 1929.

Photographs of elaborate traditional forged ornamental ironwork in Italy.

Poore, Patricia and Labine, Clem, eds.
The Old House Journal New Compendium: A Complete How-To Guide for Sensitive Rehabilitation.
Garden City, N.Y.: Dolphin Books, 1983.

A collection of techniques and materials for restoring old houses; includes a brief section on iron fences and cast iron repairs.

Robertson, Edward Graeme
Victorian Heritage: Ornamental Cast Iron in Architecture.
Melbourne, Australia: Georgian House, 1960.

Many photographs of the cast ironwork in Melbourne.

Robertson, Edward Graeme and Joan
Cast Iron Decoration: A World Survey.
New York: Whitney Library of Design, 1977.

Photos of antique cast iron.

Robins, Frederick William
The Smith: The Traditions and Lore of an Ancient Craft.
London and New York: Rider, 1953.

Social history of the smith.

Scheel, Hans
Schmiede- und Schlosserarbeiten.
Stuttgart: J. Hoffmann, 1959.

Interesting contemporary German wrought iron patterns.

Schmirler, Otto
The Art of Wrought Metalwork for House and Garden.
New York: Architectural Book Publishing Company, 1979.

Drawings and photographs of twentieth-century Austrian ironwork by the author.

Simmons, Marc and Turley, Frank
Southwestern Colonial Ironwork: The Spanish Blacksmithing Tradition from Texas to California.
Santa Fe: Museum of New Mexico Press, c. 1980.

Sonn, Albert H.
Early American Wrought Iron.
New York: Charles Scribner's Sons, 1928.

Pencil drawings of tools and other small pieces. Volume III is the only volume to deal with fences, gates, and balconies.

Underwood, Austin
Creative Wrought Ironwork.
Princeton: van Nostrand, 1965.

Good for technique, but elementary; has photos; designs are unacceptable.

Waite, Diana S.
Ornamental Ironwork: Two Centuries of Craftsmanship in Albany and Troy, New York.
Albany: Mount Ida Press, 1990.

An illustrated history of architectural ironwork in Albany and Troy.

Wallace, Philip B.
Colonial Ironwork in Old Philadelphia: The Craftsmanship of the Early Days of the Republic.
New York: Architectural Book Publishing Co., 1930.

Photos and measured drawings of ironwork.

Weygens, Alexander G.
The Modern Blacksmith.
Princeton: van Nostrand Reinhold, 1974.

Paperback book on techniques and tools.

Whitaker, Francis
The Blacksmith's Cookbook: Recipes in Iron.
Vail, Colo.: Jim Fleming Publications, 1986.

Advanced blacksmithing techniques.

Wilson, Samuel Jr. and Lemann, Bernard
New Orleans Architecture. Volume One: The Lower Garden District.
Gretna, La.: Friends of the Cabildo, 1971.

Winslow Brothers Companies
Ornamental Iron.
Chicago, 1894.

Photographs of work by this company.

Wood and Perot
Wood and Perot's Portfolio of Original Designs of Iron Railing, Verandas, Settees, Chairs, Tables, and Other Ornamental Ironwork.
Philadelphia, 1858.

A lavish, large book with excellent illustrations of designs produced by this company.

Index

About the Authors

SUSAN and MICHAEL SOUTHWORTH have practiced urban design, planning, and architecture in Boston, as well as in the San Francisco Bay area where Michael is a professor of urban design and planning at the University of California at Berkeley. Much of their work has dealt with preservation and adaptation of older towns and buildings to contemporary needs, as well as the design of urban discovery trails and information systems. Among their award-winning projects was the conceptual plan for the Urban National Park in Lowell, Massachusetts, a plan to revitalize America's first planned industrial community as an educative environment. Their ornamental ironwork commissions have included fences and gates based on a historic harpoon for the Whaling Museum in New Bedford, Massachusetts. Other books by the Southworths include the *A.I.A. Guide to Boston* (Globe Pequot Press) and *Maps* (New York Graphic Society).

The photographer, the late CHARLES C. WITHERS, was the president of The Towle Silversmiths in Newburyport, Massachusetts from 1949 to 1958, and devoted much of his life to bringing quality design into industry. In 1955 he conceived a traveling exhibition "Sculpture in Silver." He had a particular interest in encouraging a relationship of mutual service and responsibility between the artist and businessman, and organized the first "art and business" exhibitions at the Harvard Business School. For two decades he served on the Board of Directors of the Institute of Contemporary Art in Boston. He spent his leisure time photographing architectural patterns and the changing face of urban life.